STRESS LESS. LOVE LIFE MORE.

HOW TO STOP WORRYING, REDUCE ANXIETY, ELIMINATE NEGATIVE THINKING AND FIND HAPPINESS

CASSANDRA GAISFORD

CONTENTS

EXCERPT:MIND OVER MOJITOS: HOW MODERATING YOUR DRINKING CAN CHANGE YOUR LIFE

PART I

PRAISE FOR STRESS LESS. LOVE LIFE MORE

"Currently, my workload is pretty intense and a little stressful. After reading this book I felt less stressed and more focused. I highly recommend adding this helpful book to your collection."

~ Paul Brodie, Eight-time Amazon bestselling author

"This is another of Cassandra's well researched and thought provoking books, this time focusing on stress and how to best manage it. Cassandra has packed this book with great suggestions to help the reader cope with stress; brings statistics to life with colourful side stories and includes many helpful quizzes to enable the reader to gauge for themselves where their stress levels are at.

I particularly liked the Happy at Work tips. But mostly I enjoyed the way the book moved along the subject never allowing the reader to consider whether there were better books out there as this book contains everything a stressed reader, or even someone wishing to help a person who is stressed, maybe looking for in the way of practical suggestions and thought provoking information. I highly recommend this book."

~ Catherine Sloan, counselor

"Reading *Stress Less* brought me real inspiration to incorporate Cassandra's stress-busting strategies into my daily routines. While it was not news to me to read there is a correlation between reduced stress levels and self-care, meditation, and not over- "boozing," the book (and it's revealing quizzes) really drove home to me the necessity of actually putting self-care into practice.

Cassandra effectively demonstrates how high-stress is largely self-perpetuated, and anyone can become empowered to free him or herself from stress-inducing patterns and environments. *Stress Less* is well-researched, full of helpful links for further reading, listening, and exploring, and is an easily navigable resource to which I am sure I will return."

~Amy Stokes, editor

ALSO BY THE AUTHOR

Mid-Life Career Rescue:

The Call for Change
What Makes You Happy
Employ Yourself
3 Book Box Set: The Call for Change, What Makes You Happy, Employ
Yourself

The Art of Living:

How to Find Your Passion and Purpose
Career Rescue: The Art and Science of Reinventing Your Career and Life
Boost Your Self-Esteem and Confidence

The Art of Success:

Leonardo da Vinci
Coco Chanel

Journalling Prompts Series:

The Passion-Driven Business Planning Journal

Health & Happiness:

The Happy, Healthy Artist
Stress Less. Love Life More
Bounce: Overcoming Adversity, Building Resilience and Finding Joy

Mindful Sobriety:

*Mind Over Mojitos: How Moderating Your Drinking Can Change Your Life:*Easy Recipes for Happier Hours & a Joy-Filled Life
Your Beautiful Brain: Control Alcohol and Love Life More

Sexy Sobriety:

Sexy Sobriety: Alcohol and Guilt-Free Drinks You'll Love: Easy Recipes for Happier Hours & a Joy-Filled Life
The Sobriety Journal
Sexy Sobriety Two Book Bundle-Box Set: Alcohol and Guilt-Free Drinks You'll Love & The Sobriety Journal

Money Manifestation:

Financial Rescue: The Total Money Makeover: Create Wealth, Reduce Debt & Gain Freedom

The Prosperous Author:

Developing a Millionaire Mindset
Productivity Hacks: Do Less & Make More
The Prosperous Author-Two Book Bundle-Box Set (Books 1-2)

More of Cassandra's practical and inspiring workbooks on a range of career and life enhancing topics can be found on her website (www.cassandragaisford.com) and here —Author.to/CassandraGaisford

FREE WORKBOOK!

Thank you for your interest in my new book.

To show my appreciation, I'm excited to be giving you another book for FREE!

Download the free *Find Your Passion Workbook* here: http://worklifesolutions.leadpages.co/free-find-your-passion-workbook.

I hope you enjoy it—it's dedicated to helping you live and work with passion, resilience and joy.

DEDICATION

The tiny, brilliantly colorful hummingbird
symbolizes the messages in this book.

This versatile soul, despite its size,
is capable of unbelievable feats.
It can hover in mid-air, fly forwards, backwards,
side-ways, and even upside down.
Its rapidly beating wings can flap as high as 200 times per second,
enabling it to travel faster than a car.

The laws of physics say it should be impossible.
But the hummingbird does it anyway.

I dedicate this book to those of you
who are ready to live a life more colorful,
to stress less and do what others may say cannot be done.

This book is also for Lorenzo, my Templar Knight,
who encourages and supports me
to make my dreams possible...

And for all my clients
who've shared their dreams with me,
and allowed me to help them achieve amazing feats.

Thank you for inspiring me.

PREFACE

"Man is God's plaything, and that is the best part of him. Therefore, every man and woman should live life accordingly, and play the noblest games... What, then, is the right way of living? Life must be lived as play..."

~ Plato

INTRODUCTION

"Our brains never get a break and the results can be increased stress, anxiety, insomnia and, if left unchecked, even depression. But there is something you can do - nothing."

~ Mathew Johnstone

- If your relationships are suffering...
- If you constantly feel exhausted...
- If you lack confidence or self-esteem...
- If you find the challenges of life overwhelming...
- If you'd love to stress less and live more...

...then *Stress Less. Love Life More* is exactly the right book for you— because it will show you that these challenges are a critical part of your success. The secret is knowing how to use them to your advantage, to turn your world around and achieve your goals.

Perhaps you've been feeling stressed before you downloaded this book. Or you've been unhappy at work for so long that some of the symptoms of stress, such as feelings of depression, anxiety or even anger, are really entrenched.

You may be so busy trying to juggle everything that you are unaware of how much strain you are under. Like Roger, who hates his career so much he says he hates his life. Or Jan, who can't relax, and is so busy being busy that she can't remember the last time she felt real joy.

There's no doubt modern life has become more and more stressful. Many people agree that the effect of stress is becoming harder for most to handle. The pressures of work, relationships, families, the fast pace of life and increasing demands on our time can leave us in a state of turmoil.

There are two reasons: Most people have way too many demands in their lives. They're working too many hours and/or too many jobs, have too many activities, are juggling several high stress jobs while raising a family, are spending too much time in traffic, and have too many stimuli in their environment – including social media vertically hardwired to their palms (which can lead to information overload— or what I call information obesity).

Secondly, environmental toxins and poor diet are exhausting the endocrine system—particularly the adrenal glands. The adrenal glands are one of the main organs involved in the fight or flight stress response.

Diets that are high in sugar, white flour, refined foods, pesticides, and additives, and that are low in nutrients, lead to many health conditions including a malfunctioning endocrine system and depleted adrenal glands. The human body was not designed to handle the onslaught of environmental toxins we all live with daily and this puts excessive burden on the endocrine organs.

When your endocrine system is not functioning properly, you can't cope with stress effectively. This results in a vicious cycle where the weakened endocrine system creates more stress and the higher levels of stress continuously weaken the endocrine system even more.

People who are overstressed complain of being tired but unable to fall asleep or enjoy a restful night's sleep. They have plagues of aches and pains, lack of energy, and can't remember what makes them feel truly happy. They feel depressed, anxious, tearful, snappy and irritable, or just unable to cope with life.

Many people soldier on ignoring the signs their bodies are giving them. Some live to tell their stories and the lessons they learned. I was so stressed and unhappy at work many years ago, I got shingles. Others aren't so "lucky." One of my colleagues suffered a heart attack and later died.

Stress is an invisible killer, and the underlying cause of mental illness, depression and suicide. It's that serious—no wonder the onus on employers to help employees manage stress has been written into health and safety legislation. But don't rely on anyone else to be proactive about your well-being. You know that, right? That's why you picked up this book.

It's impossible to completely eradicate stress, nor would you want to; a certain amount is necessary and healthy. The solution is to reduce as much as possible and then find ways to cope with and manage the stress that can't be removed.

Listen to Your Body Barometer

You, and those you love, can be helped to avoid too much bad "stress" and build greater resilience to avoid illness and burnout. You'll do this by heeding the early warning signs and building stress-busting immunity.

By nipping your stressors in the bud before they go to seed, you will avoid wreaking havoc on your body, mind and spirit.

You'll also avoid derailing your career and damaging your relationships. Increasing your coping skills can also be a wonder cure for dissatisfaction with your work, or your life.

I'm passionate about helping people live prosperous, successful lives, and I care about your health and well-being. Stress-free people are happier people and happier people make happier communities.

I hope this book provides some helpful insights and strategies to help you manage your stress levels through any current and future demands you may be experiencing. You'll find strategies that I've used successfully, personally and professionally to whip stress into shape and enjoy life more.

Before we continue, there's just one thing you need to know. The tools I'll share in these pages are powerful solutions regardless of your goals, profession, skills, experience, age, and current situation.

They're a seamless blend of ancient wisdom and modern science. They are timeless and limitless, so it's never, ever "too late" or "too soon".

So... are you ready? Are you ready to dramatically improve your financial success and personal fulfilment? If you've gotten this far, I think you are...

HOW TO USE THIS BOOK

"He who is of a calm and happy nature will hardly feel the pressure of age."

~ Plato

Throughout *Stress less. Love Life More* you'll find a range of solutions to help you stress less and love life more. No two people will be experiencing the same levels of stress and overwhelm in their lives. You may need a lot of help, or you may need a little.

As you read through the following strategies you may find that just one or two really speak to you, and that's all the help you need.

As one advance reader wrote to me, "I cold-turkey stopped inbibing alcohol and cola and I've gained twenty years in energy."

Another person was facing a tsunami of stress and benefitted from applying a raft of stress-reduction techniques.

"I wish I had the valuable information that *Stress less. Love Life More* laid out 15 years ago when I went through a 'brown out', one step before complete 'burn out.' If I knew what physical signs to look for I would have left that job way earlier than I did. Unfortunately for me I learned the hard way what a stressful job situation can do to you both mentally and physically, but you don't have to. Instead, you just need to read this book, and follow the advice of Ms. Gaisford."

Think of this book like a shot of espresso. Sometimes one quick hit is all it takes to get started. But sometimes you need a few shots to sustain your energy. Or maybe you need a bigger motivational hit and then you're on your way. Very often, you'll want to return again and again to keep your energy levels high.

You're in control of what you need and what works best for you. Go at your own pace, but resist over-caffeinating. A little bit of guidance here-and-there can do as much to fast-track your success as consuming everything in one hit.

Skim to sections that are most relevant to you, and return to familiar ground to reinforce home-truths.

Call to Action

Apply the strategies which follow by journaling your responses to the questions and challenges presented at the end of each chapter.

"I love your works to date—provocative and supportive at the same time," a gentleman who read my *Mid-Life Career Rescue* books wrote to me.

To provoke is to incite or stimulate. It's the reason I've included open-ended questions and calls to action in each guide. The best questions are open, generative ones that don't allow for "yes/no" answers; rather, they encourage you to tap into your higher wisdom and intuition, or to go in search of answers—as successful people do.

"I really like the questions as the end of each chapter—'Call to Action.' They challenge my thinking; they provide me with opportunities to move forward," a reader of this book wrote to me.

Expand Your Learning—Follow My Blog

Dive deeper into some of the insights I've shared and signup to my newsletter and follow my blog—navigate to www.cassandragaisford.com

Re-Read My Other Books

Have you ever been guilty of skipping over the exercises in a book or failing to experiment and try some of its tips and strategies methods? I know I have.

That's why I think you should re-read not just my books, but any others you found inspiring. If job stress is getting you down, for example, *Mid-life Career Rescue: The Call for Change* will show you how to confidently leave a job you hate and start living a life you love, before it's too late.

Click the following link to go to my Amazon author's page and remind yourself of the books you've already read—or would love to read—Author.to/CassandraGaisford.

Inspirational Quotes to Support and Empower

Sometimes all it takes is one encouraging word, one timely bit of advice to awaken your power within. Throughout, I've added a variety of short sound-bites of wisdom—choosing from a wide range of super-capable men and women, historical and current, young and old.

They are men and women who share your dreams and had to overcome significant obstacles on the way to overcome stress.

Be Empowered

Empowerment is defined as giving power or authority to someone or something—who better to decide who assumes this power and sovereign authority than you?

Empowered people do what they need to do to assume mastery over their thoughts, feelings, emotions and things that affect their lives.

Empowered people are successful people because they live life on their terms. They do the things that really matter to them and those they love.

Empowered people are resilient in the face of setbacks, disappointments or attacks and they're flexible enough to tackle obstacles in their paths.

They recognize they are the experts and sovereign authority in their lives. They learn from, and surround themselves with, other empowered, successful people. They back themselves even when they don't succeed.

Are you ready to heed the call for health, happiness, and joy?

Let's get going...

Before we get into discussing solutions let's look at the impact of modern day stress and then take a closer look at just what stress is—and isn't. But first, I just wanted to let you know...one of the most effective solutions is to get help from a pro...

THE IMPACT OF MODERN DAY STRESS

Some alarming facts:

- Work related stress is a major cause of depression and it is estimated that workers with depression cost US Employers an estimated $44 billion yearly in lost productive time
- Stress is one of the leading causes of disability and mental illness. Most claims related to stress responses usually involve long absences away from work prior to the claim. In 2014, the average cost of a stress claim was $29,042, compared with $8,498 for overuse injuries, and $4,241 for back injuries
- Workers who report high stress are 30 per cent more likely to have accidents than those with low stress
- Violence at work is a growing problem: in the EU, 3 million workers reported being subjected to sexual harassment, 6 million to physical violence, and 12 million to intimidation and psychological violence
- Lack of career goals and career dissatisfaction are common causes of stress. Surveys completed by

TMP/Hudson consistently report that over 43% of the working population are dissatisfied in their work

- One Canadian study argued that a 1% improvement through helping people become fully engaged in programs that lead them to find work they would love would release an additional $600 million each year into the economy
- A recent survey revealed that NZ organizations are spending in excess of $18m per year settling personal grievances arising out of employee restructuring, performance management, and claims brought under our stress legislation laws
- Increasing numbers of organizations are investing in holistic services that help employees achieve greater work/life balance, self-esteem and wellness - realizing 5-10 times the return on investment in terms of greater productivity, increased retention of staff, reduced levels of stress, and improved succession planning

Some stress is normal

Stress is something we all feel every day. It isn't something that only happens when we're under particular pressure. Some mild stress is good for you. It gives you more energy to achieve your goals and a feeling of excitement that makes you want to succeed. The right amount of stress reminds us that we're alive.

Too much stress, however, can do the opposite. Stress that goes on for too long, or which cumulatively builds up, can make you sick. Too much stress can give you chronic headaches, affect your blood pressure, and contribute to ulcers and heart disease. Stress is also a major cause of mental illness and disability.

DEFINING STRESS

"Stress is the reaction people have to excessive pressures or other types of demands placed upon them. It arises when they worry that they can't cope."

~ NZ Department of Occupational Safety and Health

Stress versus strain

The literature of the last hundred years offers many definitions of what stress is, whether used by psychologists, doctors, management consultants or lay people. Even Hans Selye, the physician who did the pioneering research on 'stress' in the 1950's, later apologized for choosing the word "stress" to describe his findings.

For many years, Selye wrote and spoke about what he called "biological stress". After he retired, however, he confessed in his memoirs that he had used the wrong term to describe how the body's adaptive resources become exhausted.

"In seeking a name for my theory, I borrowed a term from physics, where "stress" refers to the interaction between a force and the resistance to it. I merely added an adjective to emphasise that I was using the term in a special sense, and baptised my (conceptual) child "biological stress". But frankly, when I made this choice I did not know the difference between "stress"' versus "strain".

In physics, "stress" refers to an agent, which acts upon a resistant body attempting to deform it. Whereas "strain" indicates the changes that are induced in the affected object. Consequently I should have called my findings the "strain syndrome." I did not distinguish between the causative agent and its effect upon the body." ~ Hans Selye.

(Source: Dr Al Siebert, How to Survive and Thrive in Any Life Crisis).

A modern definition

Now, one of the most commonly accepted definitions of stress is: "Stress is a condition or feeling experienced when a person perceives that demands exceed the personal and social resources that the individual is able to mobilise." (Mainly attributed to Richard S. Lazaraus).

Similarly, New Zealand's Department of Occupational Safety and Health defines stress as:

"Stress is the reaction people have to excessive pressures or other types of demands placed upon them. It arises when they worry that they can't cope."

In other words—you feel "stressed" when you don't *think* you can cope. One of the best ways to manage stress is to maximize your coping skills and build greater resilience. In the following chapters, we'll explore some simple, yet powerfully effective solutions. But first, let's look at the biology of stress.

By better understanding how the stress response works, you'll be forewarned and better able to listen to the early warning signs, take preventative action, and avoid burnout.

In the next chapter, you'll also discover how too much stress can undermine your performance. My clients often tell me that when they realize how working harder is not smarter, this motivates them to make more effective and life enhancing choices.

THE BIOLOGY OF STRESS

Instinctive stress responses and the role of hormones
There are two types of instinctive stress responses that are important to our understanding of stress and stress management: the short-term **"Fight-or-Flight"** response and the longer-term **"General Adaptation Syndrome."**

1. The **"Fight-or-Flight"** response. This is a basic biological survival instinct. When someone experiences a shock or perceives a threat, his or her body quickly releases hormones that are designed to help it survive. These "stress" hormones help us to run harder and faster – hopefully outrunning what ever is threatening us. Stress hormones serve many purposes:
2. They increase heart rate and blood pressure, delivering more oxygen and blood sugar to power important muscles.
3. They increase sweating in an effort to cool these muscles, and help them stay efficient.
4. They divert blood away from the skin to the core of our bodies, reducing blood loss if we are wounded.

5. They focus our attention on the threat to the exclusion of everything else.
6. All of this significantly improves our ability to **survive life threatening events**

If the body is exposed to these high levels of hormones and neurotransmitters on a continuous basis, then it eventually leads to malfunctioning in the brain, endocrine system, nervous system and metabolic system. Over time these hormones and neurotransmitters become depleted as they are exposed to overstimulation for too long and result in a variety of detrimental health effects.

Cortisol is your primary hormone needed for coping with stress, and if it becomes too low, then your capacity to cope with stress is impaired, which then causes even more stress.

What triggers the Fight-or-Flight response?

Research shows that we experience the fight-or-flight response simply when dealing with something unexpected. The situation does not have to be dramatic –and very rarely is it life threatening.

People can also experience this response when frustrated or interrupted, or when they experience a situation that is new or in some way challenging.

Negative consequences of the fight-or-flight response

- In this state we are excitable, anxious, jumpy, and irritable. This reduces our ability to work effectively with other people.
- With a trembling, pounding heart, we can find it difficult to execute precise, controlled skills.
- The intensity of our focus on survival can make it difficult to pay attention to other events around us, and to make fine judgements that require drawing information from other sources.
- We can find that we are accident-prone and less able to make good decisions.

There are very few situations in modern life where this response is useful. Most situations benefit from a calm, rational, controlled, and socially-sensitive approach. Further on in this workbook, we will look at some techniques to keep this fight-or-flight response under control.

1. The longer term **"General Adaptation Syndrome"** and **Burnout.** This refers to the way we learn to "adapt" to the long-term effects of exposure to stress.

When pushed to extremes people have been found to react in three stages:

First, in the *Alarm Phrase,* they react to the stressor.

Next, in the *Resistance Phrase*, they learn to adapt to, or cope with, the stressor. This phrase lasts for as long as people can support their heightened resistance.

Finally, when resistance is exhausted, people enter the *Exhaustion Phrase*, and their ability to resist declines substantially.

Burnout

"Burnout occurs when passionate, committed people become deeply disillusioned with a job or career from which they have previously derived much of their identity and meaning. It comes as the things that inspire passion and enthusiasm are stripped away, and tedious or unpleasant things crowd in."

~ Mindtools.com

In the business environment, this exhaustion contributes to what is commonly referred to as "burnout."

The classic example comes from the Wall Street Trading Floor—

by most people's standards, life on the trading floor is stressful. Traders learn to adapt to the daily stressors of big financial decisions, and the winning and losing of money.

In many cases, however, these stresses increase and fatigue starts to set in.

At the same time, as traders become more successful and earn more and more money, their financial motivation to succeed can diminish. Ultimately, many traders then experience "burnout."

"People should not put their work above everything else, but put time and energy into their families, hobbies, and social activities." Professor Linden, stress expert, claims this is the only cure for a new epidemic sweeping through workplaces around the world—Post-Traumatic Embitterment Disorder.

This disorder covers every possible gripe people have about their work and their workplaces. Yet the culprit is often not the work but the over-focus and over-importance people have placed on it.

Reactions to Stress

Fight, Flight, or Freeze Response to Stress

Modern day stress experts have renamed the "fight or flight response." It's now called the "fight, flight, or freeze response." This recognizes the fact that instead of fighting or fleeing, sometimes we tend to freeze in stressful and traumatic situations.

It also recognizes the fact that in many cases, especially in the workplace, we can't react physically by fighting or running away from the things or people who stress us out.

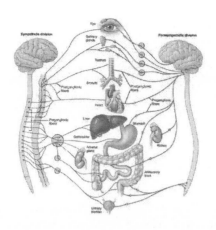

The Autonomic Nervous System

This graphic shows both the sympathetic branch, which revs us up to fight or flee and the parasympathetic branch which calms us down to rest and digest. The parasympathetic branch also coordinates the freeze response.

Understanding how the two branches of the autonomic nervous system work will help you understand the fight, flight, or freeze response. The autonomic nervous system is a network of nerve fibers that runs throughout the body, connecting the brain with various organs and muscle groups in order to coordinate the two branches of this response.

The sympathetic branch activates the fight or flight response. It tells the heart to beat faster, the muscles to tense, the eyes to dilate and the mucous membranes to dry up. All so you can fight harder, run faster, see better and breathe easier than you would without this response. And remember, this response kicks in for real threats and imagined ones in as little as 1/20th of a second: less than the amount of time between two beats of the heart.

The parasympathetic branch activates the relaxation response.

It tells the body, OK, you can relax now. The danger has passed. No need to be on alert anymore. Ideally, both work in harmony with each other to deal with the threats we face and then help us calm down and recover.

Whenever we yawn, or stretch or feel our muscles relaxing, this is the work of the parasympathetic branch. When we go to bed at night and turn off the lights, we are depending on the parasympathetic branch to kick in and allow us to sleep.

Three most serious and common effects from long-term stress

The three most serious and common effects from long-term stress are adrenal fatigue, neurotransmitter imbalances or deficiencies, and hormone imbalances.

Each of these conditions leads to another long list of debilitating symptoms including: depression, anxiety, inability to lose weight, hyperactivity, declining cognitive abilities, insomnia, chronic pain, excessive fatigue, allergies, addiction, hypoglycemia, type 2 diabetes, obesity, and cardiovascular disease.

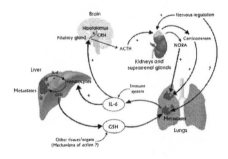

Neurotransmitters play a vital role in overseeing practically all systems and functions of the human body, like our mental and cognitive functioning, weight regulation, sleep patterns, appetite, perception of pain and pleasure and our moods.

When homeostasis is not maintained, then a variety of psychological and physiological disturbances occur. Those with an imbalance of neurotransmitters are at extremely high risk of addiction to drugs, alcohol, nicotine, caffeine, sugar, and carbohydrates.

The adrenal glands, along with the hypothalamus and pituitary, are one of the main organs involved in the stress response system. If they are not functioning adequately, then the ability to cope with stress adequately is lost. Adrenal fatigue occurs when the adrenal glands become exhausted from too much stress and they no longer perform their functions as required, which leads to problems in regulating blood sugar, the immune system, inflammation, blood pressure, managing stress, and fatigue.

This leaves people vulnerable to chronic pain disorders, chronic fatigue, allergies, immune system conditions, asthma, addiction, and many more ailments.

Hormones also play a crucial part in regulating our psychological and physical health. Mood, metabolism, mental and cognitive function, and sexual function and development are all extremely sensitive to high levels of stress. When hormones are thrown out of balance by stress, numerous disruptive, and sometimes debilitating, symptoms can occur.

Some of the most common effects of stress on the body include: anxiety, headaches, moodiness, memory loss, inability to concentrate, aggressive behavior, back pain, upset stomach, disturbed sleep, respiratory interference, and even hair loss. However, hair loss can occur for a variety of other reasons, such as low thyroid and heavy metals, so it's important not to assume your hair loss is the result of stress without ruling out other causes.

One of the most well-known and widely researched effects of stress on the body is that related to the heart and the ability of stress to contribute to coronary artery disease, high blood pressure, chest pain, or even irregular heartbeat.

Another of the most significant effects is that stress suppresses and weakens the immune system. This leaves your body vulnerable to colds, flu, and many other possible health conditions.

The body's reaction to stress also lowers your body's white blood cell count, which reduces your system's ability to heal itself. Additionally, acute stress will aggravate any pre-existing respiratory conditions such as asthma. Accumulated stress can be fatal. Yes, it's that serious!

The Stress Curve

Cumulatively high levels of stress over a period of time will push people onto the far side of the stress curve, affecting their ability to deal with complex or difficult tasks.

As a result, performance will progressively diminish and health will be compromised. This is why it's so important to find ways to stress less and relax more.

But many people have a mistaken belief that if they're not active, they're not productive. As you'll see below, high levels of stress negatively impact performance.

How stress affects performance

Important to note, many people are surprised to discover that low stimulation and boredom can be just as stressful as high stress and over-stimulation.

Like Goldilocks and the bears' porridge, the ideal is to find something that feels "just right."

Just right stress = Optimal performance

- Alert
- Rational
- Intuitive
- Inspired
- Happy
- Motivated
- Productive
- Effective

Over-stress = Diminished ability

- Anxiety
- Depression
- Irrational thinking
- Negativity
- Depression
- Exhaustion
- Panic
- Anger/violence
- Apathy

Low pressure = Boredom and fatigue

How much self-care do you exercise? Take the Self-Care Check questionnaire on the following page.

SELF-CARE CHECK

Call to Action: Self-Care Check-Up

The aim of this check-up is to develop awareness of current lifestyle factors to see if there are issues that model un-wellness. Read each item and give it a rating depending on how often the item applies to you NOW.

1. = almost always 2. = often 3. = sometimes 4. = occasionally 5. = almost never

1. You get at least two balanced meals a day

2. You get seven-eight hours sleep at least four nights per week

3. You receive affection regularly

4. You have at least one relative/friend within 50kms on whom I can rely

5. You exercise to the point of perspiration at least twice a week

6. You smoke less than five cigarettes a day *(non-smokers score 1)*

7. You take fewer than five alcoholic drinks a week *(non-drinkers score 1)*

8. Your weight is OK from a health point of view

9. Your income is adequate to meet basic expenses

10. You gain strength from your beliefs and feel comfortable with your views of the universe and your place in it

11. You attend social activities regularly

12. You have a network of friends and acquaintances

13. You have friends to confide in personally and deeply

14. You are in good health

15. You are able to be open about your feelings

16. You have intimate conversations with people you live with

17. You do something for fun at least once a week

18. You are able to organize your time effectively

19. You drink fewer than three cups of coffee, tea, Coke, or caffeinated drinks a day

20. You take quiet times for yourself during the day

TOTAL

A general picture of your Self Care status will emerge from this scale:

Less than 40—Indicates great self-care, good modeling for others
    41 to 60—Fairly good self-care
    61 to 70—Talking health but modeling sickness
    71 plus—Stop helping for a while. Do some personal work.

Any items with a score of 3, 4 or 5 suggest that you may need to re-evaluate this area of your life. You will probably need to make some changes.

In the next section you'll explore the impact of many of the stressors you face as part of normal life. You'll quickly see their cumulative toll of both happy and not so happy experiences.

SUMMARY OF RECENT EXPERIENCES

The Summary of Recent Experiences (SRE) is a table showing the 42 most important stresses that people experience in normal life. It is a great tool to help you assess cumulative stressors and to gain awareness of the impact of longer-term stress.

The SRE was developed by Dr Thomas Holmes and his fellow researchers in a series of studies that compared patients' health outcomes with the life events they had recently experienced.

In Dr Holmes' study people with a score of less than 150 had a low likelihood (30%) of illness in the near future, while those with a score of over 300 had a very high (80%) likelihood of illness.

Call to Action: Summary of Your Recent Experiences

To use the tool, work through this list of life stresses, identifying those that you have experienced in the last 12 months. As you work through, enter the number of times that the event has occurred in the last year in the "Number of Times" column.

If an event has happened more than four times during the year, give it a score of 4. For example, if you have been fortunate enough to go on vacation five times during the year, enter "4" in row 37.

When calculating this manually, multiply the number of times the event has happened by the number in the "Mean Value" column. This gives you your score for that event type. Total this to give your score.

In the example above, you will suffer a score of 52 points on the SRE if you go on holiday five times in a year.

Table: Summary of Recent Experiences

For each event listed below multiply by the value given to determine your score

1. A lot more or a lot less trouble with the boss.

X 23 =

2. A major change in sleeping habits (sleeping a lot more or a lost less or a change in time of day when you sleep).

X 16 =

3. A major change in eating habits (eating a lot more or a lot less or very different meal hours or surroundings).

X 15 =

4. A revision of personal habits (dress, manners, associations, and so on).

X 24 =

5. A major change in your usual type or amount of recreation.

X 19 =

6. A major change in your social activities (e.g., clubs, dancing, movies, visiting, and so on).

X 18 =

7. A major change in church or spiritual activities (attending/practicing a lot more or less than usual).

X 19 =

8. A major change in the number of family get-togethers (a lot more or a lot fewer than usual)

X 15 =

9. A major change in your financial state (a lot worse off or a lot better off).

X 38 =

10. Trouble with in-laws.

X 29 =

11. A major change in the number of arguments with spouse (a lot more or a lot fewer than usual regarding child rearing, personal habits, and so on).

X 35 =

12. Sexual difficulties.

X 39 =

13. Major personal injury or illness.
    X 53 =

14. Death of a close family member (other than spouse).
    X 63 =

15. Death of spouse.
    X 100 =

16. Death of a close friend.
    X 37 =

17. Gaining a new family member (through birth, adoption, oldster moving in and so on).
    X 39 =

18. Major change in the health or behavior of a family member.
    X 44 =

19. Change in residence.
    X 20 =

20. Detention in jailor other institution
    X 63 =

21. Minor violations of the law (traffic tickets, jaywalking, disturbing the peace, and so on).

X 11 =

22. Major business re-adjustment (merger, reorganization, bankruptcy, and so on).

X 39 =

23. Marriage.

X 50 =

24. Divorce.

X 73 =

25. Marital separation from spouse.

X 65 =

26. Outstanding personal achievement.

X 28 =

27. Son or daughter leaving home (marriage, attending college, and so on).

X 29 =

28. Retirement from work.

X 45 =

29. Major change in working hours or conditions.
     X 20 =

30. Major change in responsibilities at work (promotion, demotion or lateral transfer).
     X 29 =

32. Major change in living conditions (building a new home or remodelling, deterioration of home or neighborhood).
     X 25 =

33. Spouse beginning or ceasing to work outside the home.
     X 26 =

34. Taking out a mortgage or loan for a major purchase (purchasing a home or business, and so on).
     X 31 =

35. Taking out a loan for a lesser purchase (a car, TV, freezer, and so on).
     X 17 =

36. Foreclosure on a mortgage or loan.
     X 30 =

37. Vacation.

   X 13 =

38. Changing to a new school.

   X 20 =

39. Changing to a different line of work.

   X 36 =

40. Beginning or ceasing formal schooling.

   X 26 =

41. Marital reconciliation with mate.

   X 45 =

42. Pregnancy.

   X 40 =

Total Score

Interpreting the results:

Different people cope in different ways, and to a different extent. However, scores of 200 or more on this scale may show that you are experiencing high levels of longer-term stress.

You may be in danger of burning out, or of negatively affecting your health. This is particularly the case if your work is routinely stressful. Scores of 300 or more mean that you should take particular care of yourself.

Heed the warning and gain greater awareness of the signs and symptoms of stress. In the following pages, you'll discover many of the physical, emotional, cognitive, behavioral, social and cognitive signs of stress.

SIGNS AND SYMPTOMS

"Stress can cause severe health problems and in extreme cases, can cause death. Stress management techniques are conclusively shown to have a positive effect on reducing stress."

~ Mindtools.com

Physical signs of stress

- Increased heart rate
- Pounding heart
- Sweaty palms
- Elevated blood pressure
- Tightness of the chest, neck, jaw and back muscles
- Headache
- Diarrhea
- Constipation

- Unable to pass urine or incontinence
- Trembling
- Twitching
- Stuttering and other speech difficulties
- Nausea
- Vomiting
- Sleep disturbances
- Fatigue
- Being easily startled
- Shallow, rapid breathing
- Dryness of mouth or throat
- Cold hands
- Susceptibility to minor illnesses
- Itching
- Chronic pain
- Sore eyes

Emotional signs of stress

- Tearful
- Impatience
- Frightened
- Moody
- Highs and lows
- Feeling of loss/grief
- Depression
- Anger
- Irritability
- Short-tempered
- Anxiety
- Rage
- Critical

Cognitive signs of stress

- Forgetfulness
- Preoccupation
- Errors in judging distance/space
- Diminished or exaggerated fantasy life
- Reduced creativity
- Lack of concentration
- Diminished productivity
- Lack of attention to detail
- Orientation to the past
- Diminished reaction time
- Clumsiness
- Disorganization of thoughts
- Negative self-esteem
- Negative self-statements
- Diminished sense of meaning in life
- Lack of control/need for too much control
- Negative evaluation of experiences

Behavioral signs of stress

- Carelessness
- Under-eating – leading to excessive weight loss
- Over-eating – leading to weight gain
- Aggressiveness
- Increased smoking/starting smoking
- Withdrawal
- Argumentative

- Increased alcohol or drug use
- Listlessness
- Hostility
- Accident prone
- Nervous laughter
- Compulsive behavior
- Impatience
- Agitation

Social signs of stress

- Relationship difficulties
- Increased conflicts
- Marital issues
- Alienation/withdrawal
- Domestic violence

Spiritual signs of stress

- Hopelessness
- Doubting of values and beliefs
- Withdrawing from fellowship or group support
- Decreased spiritual practices (i.e. prayer, meditation, yoga etc)
- Becoming angry or bitter at a higher power or God
- Loss of compassion —for self and others

Call to Action: Heed the Early Warning Signs

How do you know you are stressed? Read each item above and highlight any signs or symptoms of stress that you may be experiencing now.

Keep an eye out for any warning signs your body barometer may give you in the future. Proactive, not reactive, care is the best strategy.

MAXIMIZE YOUR COPING SKILLS

"Synchronistic events occur when you are committed to taking extremely good care of yourself...a divine force rallies behind you to support your decisions."

~ Cheryl Richardson, author

The modern-day challenge for each of us is strain, not stress. The world is not filled with stressors darting around like invisible piranha eating away at you. There is no stress in a situation until you feel strain. For example, whether or not a person experiences stress at work depends upon the person's perception of what is going on and the person's coping skills.

Increasing your coping skills (including personal and social resources) is therefore critical in helping you survive and thrive in what feels at times to be a tsunami of demands.

Stress-resilient people know how to maximize their coping skills and mobilize personal and social resources using a variety of techniques that we will look at in this workbook.

The following exercises will help boost your self-awareness of what stress means to you, what causes your stress, and identify some of the symptoms of stress in your life.

STRESS-BUSTING AND BOOSTING RESILIENCE

"Whether or not a person experiences stress at work depends upon the person's perception of what is going on and the person's coping skills. It is not the circumstance, it is your REACTION to it that counts."

~Dr. Al Siebert

Once again, the most common and currently accepted definition of stress is, "something that is experienced when a person perceives that demands exceed the personal and social resources that the individual is able to mobilize."

In becoming stressed, people must make two judgements:

Firstly, they must feel threatened by the situation, and secondly, they must judge whether their capabilities and resources are sufficient to meet the threat.

How stressed someone feels depends on how much damage they think the situation can do them, and how closely their resources meet the demands of the situation.

This sense of threat is rarely physical. It may, for example, involve perceived threats to our social standing, to other peoples' opinions of us, to our career prospects, or to our own deeply held values.

Just as with real threats to our survival, these perceived threats trigger the hormonal fight-or-flight response with all its negative consequences.

We will now look at practical methods for managing these stressors. Firstly by looking at some ways you can control your reactions to events, including anticipating potential stressful things before they occur and building some coping strategies around them.

Listed below are a few effective coping strategies we explore in more depth throughout this book:

- Exercise
- Take breaks during the day
- Put variety into your day
- Talk to someone
- Have a definite time off
- Take time out
- Develop skills you may need (e.g. time management, communication skills/delegation
- Quit a job you hate and find one you love
- Your Coping Tools

Call to Action: Your Coping Strategy

Choose a particularly stressful event that you got through successfully. Recall what actions you took OR what others took to get you through.

Brainstorm what actions were taken under the five headings: physical, behavioral, cognitive/perceptual (thinking), emotional, and spiritual.

Physical:

Behavioral:

Cognitive / Perceptual:

Emotional:

Spiritual:

The following pages describe just a few of the many coping tools people find helpful in counteracting current stress and building resilience for the future. At the end of this section, you'll be encouraged to apply some of these strategies and create a Stress Management and Building Resilience Plan.

1

WHAT'S STRESSING YOU OUT?

"Organs evolve in response to necessity. Therefore increase your necessity."

~ Jalad-ad-din-ai Rumi,13th Century Mystic

STRESS IS CUMULATIVE, and if it's prolonged, or you have too much on the go at once, your normal coping skills can be diminished.

Making a list of all the things that are worrying you or that are currently stressing you out is an effective way to get some control over your stress levels. Once you know who or what the culprits are you can begin to devise targeted solutions.

Gaining heightened awareness of the negative effects stress and strain are creating in your life will fuel your motivation to make positive, and at times, courageous changes.

A word of caution. **Resist making huge life decisions when you're angry.**

I knew of a man who made a dramatic change during a time of acute unhappiness. For over 15 years Martin had hated his job. When he sold his shares in his business, an opportunity to reinvent his life appeared.

But lacking awareness of his transferrable skills and alternative career options he opted for self-employment in the same career. He assumed that the added flexibility and autonomy would give him back his mojo. Four years on, he's disillusioned and angry.

"I'm a 53-year old fool. I hate what I do. I hate the person it makes me. I hate my clients: I think they're all pariahs."

In a fit of rage, he decided to close down his business, take the hit, and put his house on the market.

"I'll get on a plane and leave. I can't afford to live here," he said.

AT THE TIME, I couldn't help but wonder how different the outcome may have been if he'd been proactive or sought professional help. What if he had spent more time thinking about what else he could do with his considerable skills and talents before he quit his business? What if he'd "cut his cloth" earlier? I'm sure a more strategic, less dramatic, change and reaction decision would have been reached. One with far better consequences.

In saying that, sometimes you have to know when it's time to quit, but planning, preparation, and foresight go a long way. I guess you know that or you wouldn't be reading this book.

What's stressing you out or creating the greatest strain? Here are a few common culprits:

- Career dissatisfaction (the job itself, overwork)
- Colleagues or bosses at work
- Relationships (partner, family, children etc.)
- Health (depression, self-image, weight, illness, etc.)
- Environmental (noise, weather, chaos, etc.)
- Finances
- Values conflicts
- Uncertainty
- Change (keeping up with technology)

- Information obesity/overload
- Lack of work-life balance
- Bombardment/decision fatigue
- Cumulative stress

And these are just a few of the many things placing strain on people's well-being today.

Call to Action:

In a journal or notepad, list all the things that are currently stressing you out, and record your responses to the questions below:

What words and images come to mind as you think about the words "stress" and "strain?" How do these words and images differ when you think of feeling bliss and joy?

What are things or situations that place the greatest strain on you?

Why do they "stress you out?"

What thoughts, beliefs, and perceptions underlie your reactions?

How do you react in any of the above situations?

Where do you feel stress in your body? How does it react?

HAPPY AT WORK

"To have a path of knowledge, a path with heart makes for a joyful journey and is the only conceivable way to live. We must then think carefully about our paths before we set out on them for by the time a person discovers that his path 'has no heart,' the path is ready to kill him. At that point few of us have the courage to abandon the path, lethal as it may be, because we have invested so much in it, and to choose a new path seems so dangerous, even irresponsible. And so we continue dutifully, if joylessly along."

~ Carlos Castaneda, in his book *The Fire from Within*

Are you showing signs of job dissatisfaction? Did you wake up this morning excited to face the day ahead? Or did the thought of getting up and going to work make you wish you could stay in bed?

If Monday mornings are a low point in your week, it may be a sign that it's time for a new career.

A good place to start is to use current things getting you down as signposts to your preferred future. Sometimes in life, as in photography, you need a negative to make a positive. Confirming what's causing your job blues will help you get clear about your intentions, options and possibilities.

Perhaps you're like many of my clients and wonder whether you, not your job, are the major cause of your unhappiness. Is it your attitude? Or is it your work that's making you feel trapped? Getting clear about who you are and what you need to feel happy and fulfilled is an important step in confirming exactly which one needs to change.

Some Alarming Facts:

* Less than 10% of people are visibly living their passion. Lack of passion, and career dissatisfaction, are common causes of stress, low productivity, poor performance and plummeting levels of confidence and self-esteem.

* Lack of feedback, autocratic bosses, poor work-life balance, lack of control, values conflicts, low challenge, boredom, high workloads and interpersonal conflicts push happiness levels down on a daily basis for a large number of employees.

* We all know that smoking kills but few people know that job strain is as bad as smoking according to researchers from the Harvard School of Public Health in Boston. They concluded that too often people rely on medication to tackle the job blues but one of the most effective cures would be to tackle the job environment.

* Many people have been conditioned to expect less from the world of work, and may have narrow expectations about the wealth of opportunity that now exists.

* Unhappy people: complain more, produce less, get sick more often, worry more, have fewer creative ideas, have lower energy levels, are more pessimistic, less motivated, learn slower, make poorer decisions, have lower confidence and self-esteem, are more prone to mental illnesses, including depression, and are slower to bounce back from setbacks—and these are only some of the symptoms of unhappiness.

No wonder unhappy people are exhausted.

IF STRESS at work is the culprit, follow these happy at work tips to restore the balance:

- **Get clear about what's stressing you out.** Is it your boss? Your relationship with co-workers? Lack of appreciation or something else? Using your knowledge and clarity about what's causing your job blues will help you identify possible solutions, and tap into the powerful energy of intention to create positive changes.
- **Spend time identifying what you really need to feel fulfilled and happy at work.** Is it time for a change? Change isn't always easy. It takes a lot of planning, effort and preparation. But the results are worth it. A well-planned change brings new beginnings, fresh experiences, and a job that fulfills and energizes your life.

Jasmine, a clinical psychologist once told me, "The job's just not me. I need a new one but I don't know what I want." By listing the things she didn't like, as well as the things she enjoyed in both her current and previous roles, she was better able to identify the things which were important to her. Building this list of criteria for job satisfaction helped her narrow where to begin her search.

If, after talking to people who may be able to eliminate some of your stressors and things don't get better, sometimes acknowledging the things that you're grateful for and planning an exit strategy proves to be a winning strategy.

Diana hated her job so much the strain was beginning to take a toll. When she started her job as a designer for a large international company, she thought it was great.

But the workload was excruciating—she soon found that she was doing a job that previously needed three people. She quickly felt overloaded and drained of energy.

The pressure was getting to her and she talked of being the sickest she had ever been in her life. She shared her feelings of frustration and admitted that she spent most of her day complaining about the things she didn't like about her job with her colleagues.

When she wasn't at work she moaned to her friends and to her partner. She wished she could say, "I quit," but couldn't afford to financially. Diana felt trapped.

Diana began to wonder if her illness was a direct result of feeling at "dis-ease" with her job and sought career counseling to help her work out a cure.

I asked her how—given that she was not able to resign in the short term—she felt she could make her current work situation more bearable, even enjoyable.

She found generating ideas hard and couldn't think of any possible solutions. I encouraged her to buy a journal and write down all the things about her current job she was grateful for. This threw her a bit!

After a particularly bad day she drew up her list which included: that she was employed and had a steady wage; earned overtime for extra hours; worked close to where she lived; had access to great products and services; had six weeks paid leave; and that she liaised with international buyers and people at the top of their field that she could learn from.

After completing this list Diana said she felt immediately *"lighter"* and better about her job. She began to see what a vicious self-fulfilling cycle her negative attitude to work was having and made a conscious decision to stop talking about what she didn't like.

She vowed to only speak in positive terms or not at all. As she began to feel happier and more energized, Diana found it easier to see potential solutions to her career rut.

She put forward a proposal to redefine her job and responsibilities. This wasn't accepted by her boss, but rather than become negative and resentful Diana looked for the silver lining.

She felt that by not getting what she wanted she was being prompted to get clear about what she did want long-term and to start preparing for the time when she would leave.

She set some goals and developed an action plan to bring more passion into both her private and personal life. Knowing that she was beginning to take some positive steps to move the detrimental out of her life and make room for the positive, and choosing to see obstacles as learning experiences, made her remaining time less painful.

One year later she set up her own successful design company.

"I truly believe that absent the victim mentality, everyone— regardless of background, education, or ability—can carve out a good path for themselves in this tumultuous workplace," says Richard Bolles, author of *What Color is Your Parachute.*

CALL TO ACTION

Heed the call for change. Take control of your career and your stress levels and devote yourself to improving things for the better.

You'll find plenty of inspirational and practical strategies in my *Mid-life Career Rescue* series.

I invite you to take my Happy at Work Survey. You'll get clearer about the things most impacting you and discover some ways to move forward.

Or perhaps it's not the work itself that causes stress, but something else. In the following chapters, we'll look at some common culprits, including relationships, attitudes, perceptions, and mistaken beliefs.

That's not to say you are to blame, but often a subtle shift in how you view events, and powering up your self-care routines, can make all the difference.

3

RELATIONSHIP SUCCESS

"Realize that everything connects to everything else."

~ Leonardo da Vinci

THE HEALTH of your relationships is vital to your success. Leonardo da Vinci once said, "Marriage is like putting your hand into a bag of snakes in the hope of pulling out an eel."

Read into this what you will, but the theme is clear. Make good choices and marry well, keep your relationship in good health, or don't marry at all.

Divorce your job, your boss, your partner—anyone who is toxic to your health and happiness. Take the good with the bad, don't give up too easily, work at it and recognize that nothing is absolutely perfect.

But, if you can't make things work, be it professionally or personally, be prepared to quit. Feeling like you're always getting your head bitten off, or you're surrounded by a vat of snakes, will only increase your stress and impede your success.

CONFLICT HAPPENS

As much as we all like to get on, sometimes conflict is inevitable.

People may feel threatened by your success, they may deliberately try to thwart you, or they may misunderstand your motives and desires.

Your family and loved ones may resent the time you need to spend away from them. You may feel guilty for wanting more from your life.

As da Vinci said, the noblest pleasure is the joy of understanding. Seek first to understand, and then plan your conflict-handling strategy.

This is a message that British architect Dame Zaha Mohammad Hadid took to heart. "Women are always told, 'You're not going to make it, it's too difficult, you can't do that, don't enter this competition, you'll never win it.' They need confidence in themselves and people around them to help them to get on," she once said. Her stress-busting strategy was to remain true to her vision and do what she believed.

Sadly, however, she also believed that, "Unless you're prepared to die for your work, you're no good." She was a phenomenal architect, and, in 2004, was the first woman to receive the Pritzker Architecture Prize. However, she died far too early at 65 from a stress-related heart attack.

CALL TO ACTION

How healthy are your relationships?

Who is positively affecting your life?

Who, or what, do you need to divorce?

How sharp are your conflict resolution skills?

4

PROTECT YOUR MENTAL HEALTH

"I still have to sit down in peace."

~ J.K. Rowling

"I DIDN'T QUITE RESONATE with some sections of the book like 'health,'" an advance reader of *Developing the Millionaire Mindset* wrote to me.

Tellingly, he also wrote, "Perhaps I was in a different emotional state."

Jessie Burton, author of *The Muse and The Miniaturist*, powerfully sums up how anxiety can sneak up on you and the importance of protecting your health—mentally, emotionally, physically, and spiritually.

Below is an extract from the vivid account she shared on her blog earlier in 2017:

"I looked my mental health in the eye and did not do enough to protect it. I burned out again, I suffered dehydration and a viral infection, but far worse, my anxiety came in huge and truly awful doses and, in the end, I had to cancel a few events.

I am well aware of the places I had to cancel events, and one day, I hope to make up for that in those places. It wasn't many, but I did feel terrible.

I truly love having readers, and I did the best I could, a four-month publicity tour, two continents, five events in three days kind of thing, but by the end of September, the scrutiny and analysis, repetition and a sinking of myself led to physical damage and a deep sense of alienation, panic and an indefinable loss.

The thing I want most to do in the world is write, and I agonized that if writing led to this kind of struggle, then what was the solution?"

Balance. That is the solution. And writing, more than talking about writing."

It's too late for me to be an Elena Ferrante [an Italian novelist, best known for her *Neapolitan Novels*]. I have thought much about authority, invisibility, how to synthesize the experience of life into fiction in the best ways I can, the ways that feel truest and strongest and will make a reader go with me and say, 'yes.'

A writer's selfhood vies with her need to make herself invisible, in order to freely inhabit a simulacrum of multiple lives in fiction (aka Ferrante), and work without worrying about her own received persona in all of it.

A published writer has people pay to read the manifestations of her imagination, soul, and heart. For me, that remains extraordinary. It will always be the dream transaction for me, but it is also the most exposing, the rawest, unavoidable, supremely important fact in my life that I have battled desperately to understand and get a handle on these past three years.

It's a rockier path, certainly, knowing you are going to be held publicly accountable, knowing that your personhood will be as relevant to your artifices when it comes to talking about the work.

I know I'm not alone in this battle and I am grateful to the other writers who have spoken to me about this on the way, sometimes reaching out without me even having to ask.

My own lack of anonymity when I publish is something I am coming to accept. I handed it over without even thinking about it.

I made a pact with the kindly devil with my eyes wide shut, but I do not regret it. Having my novels bought and read has been the best thing that ever happened to me.

Sometimes, however, the things that are best for us are not always the easiest. I do regret my inability to find my pause button, but maybe writing that regret here will enable me to locate that mysterious setting inside myself?

I want to write, and write well, and that's nearly all I ever want to do."

Call to Action

How can you sustain your productivity, prepare for inevitable success and avoid overload and overwhelm?

What mental health practices would make a tremendous difference to your sustained well-being and prosperity?

You'll find a few helpful reminders and strategies in the chapters which follow.

5

CHANGE THE WAY YOU REACT

"You must take personal responsibility. You cannot change the circumstances, the seasons, or the wind, but you can change yourself. That is something you have charge of."

~ Jim Rohn, author and entrepreneur

BY CHANGE of reaction comes change of circumstance, say many great spiritual masters and teachers. If you are distressed and on the verge of burnout, taking back control can prove challenging. It is hard to feel optimistic when you are overwhelmed, depleted, and despairing.

It's hard—but not impossible. Viktor Frankl, an Austrian psychiatrist who survived the horrors of Nazi death camps, believed that it's not the situation which defines and controls us, but our attitudes and reactions. The key to his survival, Frankl maintained, was searching for meaning in that which seems unfathomable.

Stressed or not, you can determine your reaction. Ensure success at becoming less stressed by:

- Focusing on three good things you have done each day
- Praising yourself when you achieve a result
- Practicing radical acceptance of yourself, or the situation, if you feel stressed
- Find meaning and purpose in your experience. In the next chapter we'll explore how in more depth.

Throughout *Stress Less. Love Life More: How to Stop Worrying, Reduce Anxiety, Eliminate Negative Thinking and Find Happiness,* you'll discover strategies to help you transcend the biological stress reaction before it overpowers you. Listed below are two simple strategies:

Reinterpret the situation: e.g., change the meaning; instead of "they should do what I want," try, "I'm learning how to cope with other peoples' demands."

Modify or remove the stressor/s: eg., assertive action; prioritize; work reasonable hours; quit a job you hate.

6

DEALING WITH PERCEPTION

"Change the way you look at things and the things you look at change."

~ Wayne Dyer, author

THE WAY YOU VIEW EVENTS, people, and situations can create stress. A simple way to change your level of stress begins by changing how you view circumstances.

COPING STRATEGIES:

- **Reframe:** change way you see the event; e.g., when you wake up in the middle of the night, see this as extra time to read, plan, and think; see problems as challenges.
- **Look at the here and now:** what you are worrying about may never happen
- **Self-talk** - make it positive; not "I can't cope," but, "I can do

this; I've handled change before," or, " I trust myself to be able to handle this."

- **Don't think in absolutes:** you will disappoint yourself. "I must be perfect at everything I do all the time," is setting yourself up for failure.
- **It's OK to feel bad:** It is a myth that we feel good all the time
- **Don't focus on the bad:** not "The car has broken down - why me?" but, "It's a nuisance, and I'll deal with it."

Other helpful coping strategies include advance preparation. Minimize the impact of stress and boost your resilience, by:

- **Identifying stressful events in advance**
- **Avoiding** them if possible—e.g., get up earlier to avoid running late for interviews or network meetings
- **Identifying your stress reactions** so that you can pamper yourself, self-soothe or take extra self-care
- **Planning your winning strategy.** What options do you have? What is the most realistic solution?
- **Planning small, realistic steps:** don't overwhelm yourself or try to do everything you need to at once
- **Choosing a few important goals:** prioritize and accept that some things may have to be pushed back
- **Praising yourself** when you cope well. This boosts confidence and self-esteem, strengthening your ability to handle future stress

IN THE NEXT chapter you'll discover how, despite experiencing extreme stress, some of the world's most influential people have found gifts from their suffering.

7

LOOK FOR THE GIFT

"Nothing beautiful in the end comes without a measure of some pain, some frustration, some suffering."

~ His Holiness the Dalai Lama

IN *THE BOOK OF JOY*, two great spiritual teachers, the Dalai Lama and Archbishop Desmond Tutu—men who have both known tremendous suffering, encourage us all to look for the gifts contained within adversity. One of these gifts is the opportunity to be reborn.

"When I spoke about mothers and childbirth, it seems to be a wonderful metaphor, actually, that nothing beautiful in the end comes without a measure of some pain, some frustration, some suffering," writes the Dalai Lama. "This is the nature of things. This is how our universe has been made up."

In *The Book of Joy* the Dalai Lama shares how the gift of being exiled from his beloved Tibet provided the opportunity to give birth to a new way of being and to share his teachings and Buddhist philosophy throughout the world. "Life is suffering," he says. "It's how you react to life that changes your karma", he teaches. "I'm just one human being, but I believe each one of us has a responsibility to contribute to a happier humanity."

It is no coincidence that successful and revered people see the cup half full, look for ways to add more to peoples' lives rather than play the victim, and demand life treat them more favorably.

Sometimes in life, as with photography, you need the negative to develop. What at the time seemed like a low point can, with hindsight, prove to be the most life-changing and meaningful experience.

CALL TO ACTION

How might you be able to experience joy even in the face of inevitable challenges?

8

FOLLOW YOUR BLISS

"Follow your bliss and the universe will open doors where there were only walls."

~ Joseph Campbell,, mythologist and author

As I SHARED at the beginning of this book, following your bliss is a great antidote to stress. Whether you refer to the things, people and situations that fill you with happiness as sparking passion, joy, love or desire these powerful heart-felt emotions are natural opiates for your mind, body and soul.

Charles Kovess, author of *Passionate People Produce*, describes passion as: "A source of unlimited energy from the soul that enables people to achieve extraordinary results."

Often when you're feeling stressed, the things that you love to do are the first things to be traded. When you tap into something you deeply believe in and enjoy you may be amazed at the results.

Passion brings the energy or chi of love, giving you energy, vitality and a heightened sense of well-being. It's one of the greatest stressbusters of all, and promotes the generation of endorphins—feel-good chemicals that will give you an extra spring in your step. Even five minutes a day doing something you love can give you your mojo back.

What may start off as a hobby could very well turn out to be your ticket to a more fulfilling career. Like for Brian Clifford, owner of Integrated Pest Management, who had always been fascinated with bugs. After becoming disenchanted with his first career, he opted to follow his passion and became a "pestie." He loves the idea of being a white knight coming to peoples' rescue.

CALL TO ACTION

What do you love doing? What inspires you? What makes you feel joyful? Identify these things and make some time to follow your bliss.

9

CLUTTER IS THE ENEMY

"Clutter is nothing more than postponed decisions."

~ Barbara Hemphill, businesswoman

CHAOS LEADS to stress and exhaustion, ending in physical and emotional depletion. Work, family, health, finances—it often seems as though there's a never-ending pile of things to get sorted.

"With steady intent, take care of yourself, your loved ones. Make sacred the spaces around you, fulfil the duties of your life with your innate grace and kindness. This is the spirit of service. Don't underestimate the strength and importance of even your simplest actions," writes Melanie Spears, creator of *The Gratitude Diary*.

Before sitting down to write this chapter, I was incredibly frustrated. The reason? I couldn't find what I was looking for. In this instance, I was searching for the contact details of a person who had offered to proofread one of my books.

Some people are blessed with superior organizational skills—

others, like me, are gifted in other areas, like generating ideas, versatility, and adaptability.

To succeed, however, I need to stress less. You do, too. Amongst other skills you need in order to achieve success is superior organizational ability.

When faced with overwhelm, sometimes the best place to start is somewhere simple.

"Perhaps the sock drawer. Just how many mismatched socks is it possible to have? The windows, just how much brighter is that room once the dust has been removed? All simple steps, but they will yield immediate results," says Spears.

"There is a calm that can ascend when we're quietly busy with seemingly mundane tasks. Our minds are free to drift and muse, and in the spaciousness of busyness, new solutions to old problems have room to appear."

KNOW Where You're Weak

Just because something is not a natural gift doesn't mean we have to be a victim to our innate shortcomings.

Bob Mayer, *New York Times* bestselling author and the CEO of Cool Gus Publishing, gives a practical exercise in his writing workshops and suggests you look at your Myers-Briggs personality type.

For those of you who are not familiar with Myers-Briggs or the MBTI (Myers-Briggs Type Indicator), it is a personality profiling system based on Swiss psychologist Carl Jung's typological theory and developed by Katherine Cook Briggs and her daughter Isabel Briggs Myers.

In the Myers-Briggs typology system, there are sixteen personality types consisting of four letters: E for extrovert or I for introvert, S for sensor or N for intuitive, T for thinker or F for feeler, and P for perceiver or J for judger.

You can read more about Myers-Briggs here and find books about it here. Myers-Briggs typology can offer a lot of insight into how someone thinks, and, in the case of an author, how someone writes.

"Look at the opposite of your personality—this is most likely the area you need to do the most work," says bestselling author and influential blogger Kristen Lamb.

It's no surprise, having taken the test (and also being a qualified MBTI practitioner), to learn that my Myers-Briggs type is ENFP (as is Kirsten Lamb's).

I know my strengths, amongst other things, are my flexibility and adaptiveness. But with these come weaknesses—a comfort with leaving things open-ended (flexible), a resistance to committing to closure prematurely, and a love of gathering more and more information and working on multiple projects at any one time.

Take a look at my navigation bar on my browser on any one day and most likely you'll find multiple tabs open as I "research" and gather more ideas.

My opposite personality profile is ISTJ. ISTJs are naturally organized, orderly, and are energized by getting things done. They like to work systematically, completing one task before moving to the next.

This describes my partner perfectly. To say that the way I work is stressful to him is putting it mildly. But lately, I've been stressing myself out.

"ENFP (The Inspirer)—ISTJ (The Duty Fulfiller)," writes Lamb. "Together, assuming they are making use of their differing gifts and abilities for a common purpose, they make an awesome team!"

To do my best work, therefore, and stress less, I need to borrow some of his, and other ISTJs', qualities—either by borrowing their skills directly via asking for "free" help, or by copycatting my way to success. Or, I could pay for mentoring or outsource some of the organizational things I struggle with. Many authors do this successfully when they engage a Virtual Assistant.

ISTJs are systematic, orderly, structured, and disliking of diversions. They are playful—future focused, advance-planning, and preferring to make firm plans. They are early- starting—motivated by self-discipline, steady progress, and stressed by late starts.

ISTJs are scheduled, they are motivated by routines, lists, and efficient procedures. These all help them to do their best work. ISTJs are also methodical. Where an ENFP may prefer to plunge in and let strategies emerge, ISTJ's plan specific tasks, note subtasks, and thrive on organization.

THE PARETO PRINCIPLE

To again cite Kirsten Lamb, "*In Eat That Frog*, Brian Tracy also introduces the Pareto Principle. In short, 20% of our activity will account for 80% of our results.

"This means that if we have a list of ten things to do, TWO of those items will be worth as much if not more than the other eight combined.

"But can you guess which items we are most likely to procrastinate on doing? The items that will cause us the most stress and sap most of our energy? Right. The two activities that could make the most difference. We are also most likely to procrastinate where we are weak.

"Can you guess where I procrastinate? Yep, any activity that requires organizational skills. Whether it is plotting my novel or filing invoices, I do everything I can to get out of doing the chores that require I operate where I am weak. Yet, remember the rule I began with?

"Your weakest key area sets the height at which you can use all your other skills and abilities."

CALL TO ACTION

Knowledge is power. Without an inventory of strengths versus weaknesses, you can't plan a success strategy. List the issues you struggle with and identify possible ways to conquer them and minimize your stress.

Looking for things is an incredible waste of time and a massive drain of precious energy. Get organized. Spend time each day, each week, each month, developing systems to streamline your efficiency.

Declutter. Embrace the elemental art of simplicity. Remove things from your life that don't spark joy.

10

THE BALANCED LIFE

"The greatest discovery of my generation is that human beings, by changing the inner attitudes of their minds, can change the outer aspects of their lives."

~ William James, psychologist and philosopher

RESEARCH PROVES that people who organize their whole life around their work are more prone to develop Post-traumatic Embitterment Disorder – a disorder that covers almost every negative emotion a person can have at work.

On a typical day in the brain, trillions of messages are sent and received. The messages that are happy, upbeat messages are carried by the brain's "happy messengers" (scientifically known as the Biogenic Amine/Endorphin System). Other messages are somber and disquieting. They are carried by the brain's "sad messengers."

Most nerve centers receive input from both types of messengers. As long as this input is balanced, everything runs along on an even keel; however, lack of balance leads to feelings of stress.

Stress causes problems with the brain's happy messengers. When life is smooth, the happy messages keep up with demand. But when too much stress is placed on the brain, the happy messengers begin to fall behind on their deliveries.

As the stress continues, the happy messages begin to fail. Important nerve centers then receive mostly *sad messages*, and the whole brain becomes distressed. The person enters a state of brain chemical imbalance known as over-stress.

Over-stress makes people feel terrible. When sad messages overwhelm the happy messages, people can feel overwhelmed by life. They often complain of being tired, unable to fall asleep, or to obtain a restful night's sleep. They have plagues of aches and pains, lack energy, and feel less enjoyment of life. Depression, anxiety, or just feeling unable to cope with life often ensues.

Find time for the things you enjoy and prioritize the things that are most important. Isolate all the key areas of your life and check to see if you have got the balance right.

Tip the balance back into your favor by making room for the happy messages! Some simple but effective ways include:

- Noticing something beautiful every day
- Daily appreciation of things you are grateful for
- Taking time to indulge and feed your passions
- Being with people who make you feel special
- Laughing
- Hanging out with children
- Keeping a daily log of at least one thing that makes you happy

CALL TO ACTION

Have you taken too much on? If so, what can you let go of? Remember to focus on one goal at a time; then it is achievable.

11

BREATHE DEEPLY

"Under prolonged pressure, we start to chest-breathe at a faster rate. That's what readies us for action. But it also switches off the executive-functioning part of the brain."

~ Sarah Laurie, life coach

IN A STATE of joy and relaxation, you breathe in a deep circular pattern, your heart comes into coherence, and you begin to produce alpha brain waves, giving you access to your own natural tranquillizers and antidepressants.

But under stress your breathing is reversed. Instead of breathing slowly and deeply, your breathing tends to become shallower and more rapid. During times of extreme stress, you can forget to breathe at all!

You may even hyperventilate - breathing in an abnormally rapid, deep, or shallow pattern. You will exhale too much carbon dioxide, and as the level of carbon dioxide in the blood drops, the blood vessels narrow, allowing less blood to circulate. If too little blood reaches your brain, you'll become dizzy and may faint.

Calcium in the blood also decreases, causing some muscles and nerves to twitch. The twitching may result in a tingling or stabbing sensation near your mouth or in your chest. These symptoms include a tight feeling in the chest, as though your lungs cannot receive enough air.

This sensation leads to faster and deeper breathing. The heart may begin to pound, and the pulse rate may rise. Experiencing these symptoms increases anxiety in some people, which can make the condition worse.

If this happens to you, or you have forgotten how to breathe, try this: breathe in deeply for a count of four, and exhale—slowing for a count of eight. Repeat 10 times. Notice how quickly your body and mind relaxes. Try this anywhere, anytime you notice feelings of stress returning, and beat the stress response. Or tap into a meditation or yoga class for enhanced breathing practice with the added benefit of a mind-body makeover.

CALL TO ACTION

Remember to breathe! Breathing deeply can evoke a state of calm and perspective during times of stress, allowing you to cope more effectively and slow down or inhibit the stress response.

12

MOVE!

"Walking for me is my way of thinking, my way of meditating."

~ Paulo Coelho, author

MANY PEOPLE LEAD SEDENTARY LIVES, but the most successful ones praise the benefits of exercise. Many use their exercise as a time to reset and plan.

How much time do you spend outside, communing with nature? Research has shown that most people spend 90 percent of their time indoors, and most of it glued to their laptops, mobile devices, and other technology.

Vitamin D sufficiency, along with diet and exercise, has emerged as one of the most important success factors in human health.

During times of stress you can become lethargic. Feeling that you don't even have the energy or time to exercise may increase feelings of depression and irritability.

Discipline yourself to go out and get some fresh air—ideally somewhere not too frenzied.

Combine brisk walking with deep breathing to boost your energy levels, short-term memory, and state of mind.

When your breathing is calm and steady, your body is in a nurtured state which helps strengthen your immune system.

Numerous studies have shown that exercise promotes the production of positive endorphins, which play a key role in making you feel better about yourself and your capacity to cope.

In the one-sided state of depression, there is very little electrical activity in the brain. A person on a stationary bike has more electrical activity in their brain than a person watching an educational video. The truly depressed person will have such low electrical activity that making basic decisions, including the mood-enhancing decision to exercise (even just a little), becomes very difficult.

Researchers also confirm there is a strong link between breathing, outside energy, and beneficial brainwave patterns. This may explain why so many people say that walking is their meditation—clearing their minds, and allowing space for good ideas to flourish.

Getting up and moving, embracing the flow of "chi" in your entire system, will enable you to activate both hemispheres of your brain – bringing a new perspective as well as greater tolerance to life's stressors.

Getting up and moving, embracing the flow of 'chi' in your entire system will enable you to activate both hemispheres of your brain – bringing a new perspective as well as greater tolerance to life's stressors.

"It's not that I am thinking but I am in a kind of trance, totally connected with the present moment," Paulo Coelho says. When he returns to his work, his mind is clear and he is more powerfully connected to source energy.

CALL TO ACTION

Listen to your body barometer when it tells you to exercise more and sloth less.

Commit to a regular exercise regime and a more healthy diet. Be consistent so that changes easily fall into place and become life-affirming habits.

13

AVOID DECISION FATIGUE

"'What should I work on right now?' That question is a signal that you are wasting way too much time in your life."

~ Tim Morkes, author

AT WORK, we make a myriad of choices every day. Add to this the other decisions you must make in your life and it's no wonder so many of us are fatigued.

"When you go to the grocery store, do you ask yourself at every stop sign, stop light, or intersection, 'which road should I turn down?'" asks Morkes.

"No way. You either:

1. have the optimal path memorized; it's muscle memory; or, 2. you're using a GPS. In either scenario, the next step is clear. The only time you would ever ask a question like 'what next?' is if you don't know the next step of a process. That's more than okay if you're charting unknown territory...It's not okay if it's your default state."

Ask "what should I do next?" more than a few times a day and you'll burn yourself out—it's called Decision Fatigue.

So what's the solution? Tim Morkes suggests the following:

Step 1. Plan

Step 2. Prioritize

Step 3. Focus

PLANNING is all about identifying all the tasks you MUST DO in order to achieve your goal.

PRIORITIZATION is all about identifying every CRITICAL PATH task, so you do the things that will actually move the needle and get you to your goal (and won't hold up your launch, or marketing campaign, or book release, or whatever)

FOCUSING is all about accomplishing that single, most important CRITICAL PATH item daily.

So, as you look at your calendar or to-do list for today/this week/this month, ask yourself:

- What is the CRITICAL PATH to get from point a to point b?
- What is the single task that must be accomplished before I can work on the next most important task?
- Put that task in front of you and DO THAT TASK
- Wash, rinse, repeat

Simple?

Yes.

Easy?

IT DEPENDS:

- Are you getting everything done that you need to in order to move your writing projects business forward?
- Do you always accomplish your most important single daily task? (do you even HAVE a single most important daily task?)
- Are you able to "turn off" work on evenings and weekends?

As Gary Keller writes in *The One Thing: The Surprisingly Simple Truth Behind Extraordinary Results,* "YOU WANT LESS. You want fewer distractions and less on your plate. The daily barrage of e-mails, texts, tweets, messages, and meetings distract you and stress you out. The simultaneous demands of work and family are taking a toll.

"And what's the cost? Second-rate work, missed deadlines, smaller paychecks, fewer promotions--and lots of stress. AND YOU WANT MORE. You want more productivity from your work. More income for a better lifestyle. You want more satisfaction from life, and more time for yourself."

You also want less choice. I no longer ask myself, "What will I wear today?" On writing days, I have a uniform of sorts, something casual and flowing that I put on to write. I plan meals in advance so I don't face the daily grind of deciding what to eat for breakfast, lunch, and dinner. In this way, I can save my brain power for the things that improve my prosperous productivity. I wasn't born a planner, but I've begun to value it as I witness the benefits—including more energy and greater willpower.

"As it turns out, your willpower is like a muscle," writes blogger James Clear. "And similar to the muscles in your body, willpower can get fatigued when you use it over and over again. Every time you make a decision, it's like doing another rep in the gym. And similar to how your muscles get tired at the end of a workout, the strength of your willpower fades as you make more decisions."

Clear suggests 5 strategies to help reduce fatigue:

1. Plan daily decisions the night before.

For example, decisions like...

What am I going to wear to work? What should I eat for breakfast? Choices like this can be decided in 3 minutes or less the night before, which means you won't be wasting your willpower on those choices the next day. Taking time to plan out, simplify, and design the repeated daily decisions will give you more mental space to make the important choices each day.

2. Do the most important thing first.

What's the most important thing for you right now?

Is it getting in shape? Is it building your business? Is it writing that book you have inside of you? Is it learning to eliminate stress and relax?

Whatever it is for you, put your best energy toward it. If you have to wake up 30 minutes earlier, then do that. Start your day by working on the most important thing in your life.

3. Stop making decisions. Start making commitments.

I've found much more success by scheduling the things that are important to me.

For example, my schedule for writing is 9-12 Monday, Tuesday and Thursday. My schedule for marketing is Wednesday. On any given Friday, I don't have to decide whether I'm going to write. I know that's my client coaching day and it's already on the schedule. And I'm not hoping that I'll have enough willpower to meditate or write my Morning Pages. It's just what I do every day at 8 and 6.

"If you sit back and hope that you'll be able to make the right decisions each day, then you will certainly fall victim to decision fatigue and a lack of willpower," says Clear.

4. If you have to make good decisions later in the day, then eat something first.

When you want to get better decisions from your mind, put better food into your body—never decide on an empty stomach.

5. Simplify.

Do less, achieve more. Eliminate.

"Find ways to simplify your life. If something isn't important to you, eliminate it. Making decisions about unimportant things, even if you have the time to do so, isn't a benign task. It's pulling precious energy and willpower from the things that matter," says Clear.

Some of the things I've implemented to simplify my life are working on only one thing at any one time; creating systems, templates, and routines; and planning my days in advance.

I promise, if you commit to reducing the number of decisions in your life, it will make a tremendous difference to your life and your productivity.

CALL TO ACTION

Make one decision, and only one, right now—decide to do less and earn more! Stop relying on brain and will power and start developing systems and routines that become daily habits. Eliminate distractions and automate as much as you can. You'll learn how as you read this book.

14

TAKE CONTROL OF YOUR TIME

"Go after whatever gives you meaning in life and trust yourself to handle whatever it takes."

~ Kelly McGonigal, health psychologist

CONTROL YOUR TIME or it will control you. Activity logs are a great way to keep track of productive time and to see clearly where you are wasting it. Using the following log, make a list of everything you do and the time you take to do it.

Analyze it after 2-3 weeks. Identify and eliminate time-wasting and low-yield activities. Identify more efficient ways to work.

If you have multiple income streams and demands on your time, you may prefer to set up an excel sheet and color-code your activities.

I've done this recently and love it. Color coding allows me to quickly see time sucks, while monitoring holds me more personally accountable.

DATE

TIME

ACTIVITY

WAYS TO PRIORITIZE TIME:

Keep a "to do" list: break up large tasks into smaller tasks. Allocate priorities from A (very important) to F (unimportant). When you have several tasks of similar priority, number them in order of priority, i.e. B2 may be the second most important B priority task.

Delegate: Work out the value of skills and time—delegate lower value tasks to others; contract in extra resources if needed

Negotiate: Try and find a mutually agreeable solution to time demands and work required by others

Take breaks: Refresh your mind. Rather than wasting time you will gain time by being more productive.

Develop systems: Organize yourself better. This will help you avoid wasting time looking for things or reinventing the wheel.

Set key objectives: Decide what your most important goals are and what you won't compromise on achieving. Then make a plan of everything you are going to have to do to achieve these objectives. Try not to do any tasks that won't lead your directly to achieving your key objectives. Become a creative procrastinator by putting off until tomorrow that which won't advance your goals today!

Allocate and schedule: Decide what constitutes a suitable balance of work-life time for you and allocate it each week. How many hours for work? For family? For play? Set rules for yourself on how your time is used and try not to compromise.

Rest for peak performance: Working harder, not smarter, is a key reason many people are stressed. Do less and achieve more.

CALL TO ACTION
How can you take better control of your time?

15

MAGIC MORNINGS

"If you win the morning, you win the day."

~ Tim Ferriss, polymath

DESPITE HIS PHENOMENAL success Tim suffers from anxiety and credits a robust morning routine and other health behaviors with giving him more bounce throughout the day.

Ferriss kick-starts his day with 10-20 minutes of transcendental meditation, five to 10 minutes of journaling or Morning Pages, making his bed, and a healthy dose of positive vibes. He also does at least 30 seconds of light exercise. 30 seconds!

"Getting into my body, even for 30 seconds, has a dramatic effect on my mood and quiets mental chatter," Ferriss wrote in his book *Tools of Titans.*

I've followed a similar ritual for years—long before I discovered Tim Ferris. But whenever I am tempted to flag my meditation or my ritual of writing in my journal, I find it helpful to remind myself these are the tools Titans like Tim use to achieve phenomenal results.

Below are just a few of the many *Magic Morning* routines and rituals you can use to prime your day for miracles:

- Meditation and mindfulness—enjoy some sacred silence
- Affirmations—empower your beliefs with feeling-based reminders of your intentions
- Goals to go for—set your priorities, including health and well-being activities (exercise etc.)
- Inspiration—journaling, visualization, reading
- Co-create—partner with spirit, tap into your Higher Self, evoke the muse...and get ready to create

Importantly, complete these crucial focusing activities *before* you get to work.

I experience many of these activities simultaneously when I meditate, write my Morning Pages, and consult the oracles; and also when I go for a walk in nature, listen to an uplifting audiobook or podcast, or sip my morning coffee.

Ferriss, in a podcast episode, sums up the potency of similar mindful practices: "It's easy to become obsessed with pushing the ball forward as a Type-A personality and end up a perfectionist who is always future-focused.

"The five-minute journal is a therapeutic intervention, for me at least, because I am that person. That allows me to not only get more done during the day but to also feel better throughout the entire day, to be a happier person, to be a more content person—which is not something that comes naturally to me."

I'm not alone in knowing the positive difference daily habits like journaling or taking the time to reconnect with my higher self, makes to my resilience and happiness levels.

Get your day off to a high-vibration start. Choose, develop, and apply your own Magic Morning routines.

CALL TO ACTION

Consider purchasing a copy of my book *Bounce: Overcoming Adversity, Building Resilience and Finding Joy* and *Tools of Titans*. Be sure to not just read these books, but also to adopt some of the new habits you'll learn.

Choose, develop, and apply your own miracle morning routines. What secret weapons can you use to win the war of life and create an incredibly productive, stress-free routine?

16

YOUR 'NOT TO DO' LIST

"Meetings are an indicative, highly self-indulgent activity that corporations and other organisations habitually engage in only because they cannot masturbate."

~ Dave Barry, Pulitzer Prize-winning American humorist

WHEN TIM FERRISS started advising start-ups in 2008 and people asked him for advice, "Instead of answering, 'What should we do?' I tried first to hone in on answering, 'What should we simplify?'" he writes in his bestselling book, *Tools of Titans*. "Adding elements to your business strategy is often expensive and time-consuming but removing things isn't."

Ferriss says, "I've since applied this 'What if I could only subtract ...?' to my life in many areas, and I sometimes rephrase it as 'What should I put on my not-to-do list?'"

Here's some of the things many successful people vow not to do, or do less of, to stress less:

- Surfing the internet incessantly
- Playing games endlessly
- Spending too long on Facebook and social media
- Signing up for too many webinars
- Investing in over-learning
- Getting involved in extra activities
- Relentless perfectionism

Many of these activities, rather than boost productivity, deplete maximum performance.

Jessie Burton, author of *The Muse* and *The Miniaturist,* posted on one of her blogs the following "not to do's":

- I will not sleep with my phone in my room
- I will not bow to the peer pressure of being sociable. It is impossible to write and read all I want to and also be very sociable
- I will not envy the lives of others. It really is the most stupid thing in the world to do. It is so unbelievably stupid
- I will not be ashamed of my coldness. I'm learning that such admissions only make you warmer. But nevertheless, I will keep those icy little shards, because they're tremendously useful in getting you through, in seeing things, in seeing yourself.

Early in my writing career, some of the things I put on my "not to do list" included:

- Watching television
- Spending time with negative people
- Getting enmeshed in other people's dramas
- Signing up for more courses
- Procrastinating
- Over analyzing and over-thinking
- Trolling Facebook

The other thing I have become a lot better at is mastering the art of refusal.

"Be that kid," writes Tim Ferriss in *The Four-Hour Work Week*. "Learn to be difficult when it counts. In school as in life, having a reputation for being assertive will help you receive preferential treatment without having to beg or fight for it every time.

"There was always one small kid who fought like hell, thrashing and swinging for the fences. He or she might not have won, but after one or two exhausting exchanges, the bully chose not to bother him or her. It was easier to find someone else."

Be that person, urges Ferriss.

"Doing the important and ignoring the trivial is hard because so much of the world seems to conspire to force crap upon you. Fortunately, a few simple routine changes make bothering you much more painful than leaving you in peace. It's time to stop taking information abuse."

CALL TO ACTION

Identify your abusers—who or what steals productive hours from your day? Negotiate, bargain or come out arms swinging, to re-claim your power and create space for peace and joy.

17

FEED YOUR FUTURE

"The only way to keep your health is to eat what you don't want, drink what you don't like, and do what you'd rather not."

~ Mark Twain

REDUCING CAFFEINE, alcohol, nicotine and other stimulants is a powerful way to feel better during times of stress. The trouble is that these sorts of stimulants are just the things people feel drawn to.

Like John who hates his job and tries to switch off by hitting the bottle, "I'm going to get a bottle of wine. It's the only way I can cope. I can't do this work without it."

We'll look more at why reducing alcohol intake is an important stress-reduction strategy in the next chapter. In summary, it's important to knock stimulants such as caffeine, alcohol, and nicotine off your list (or at least limit your intake).

These trigger the production of the stress-related hormone adrenaline - which increases your heart rate, prompts the liver to release more sugar into your bloodstream, and makes the lungs take in more oxygen.

While these things may give you a short term high, in the long run, the end result is fatigue and low energy levels – leading to a vicious cycle of relying on more stimulants to get you through the day.

Dying for a smoke? One of my clients started smoking during a period of stress. "I was bored," she said. "I just wanted to fit in with the people I was working with."

Aside from serious health implications you know about, like lung, brain, and throat cancer, smoking robs the blood, muscles, brain and organs of oxygen, causing people to feel light-headed and tired and impeding optimal functioning.

Nicotine also increases levels of adrenaline and creates a vicious cycle of energy highs and lows. Cut down or stop. To help curb cravings, try taking a complex B vitamin supplement.

Caffeine Use Disorder

The impact of excessive coffee and caffeinated drinks has become such a health-hazard, a new disorder, Caffeine Use Disorder, was recently added to the DSM-V - the tool psychologists, psychiatrists, and other mental-health professionals often refer to prior to making their diagnosis.

Are you addicted?

If you've experienced these three symptoms within the past year - you may be in trouble:

1. You have a persistent desire to give up or cut down on caffeine use, or you've tried to do so unsuccessfully.

2. You continue to use caffeine despite knowing it contributes to recurring physical or psychological problems for you (like insomnia, or jitteriness).

3. You experience withdrawal symptoms if you don't have your usual amount of caffeine.

Many of my clients notice reduced levels of anxiety, irritability and depression when they kick the habit. They also report feeling better able to cope with stress.

But a word of warning, caffeine, like any drug, is highly addictive and you may have to suffer a little first. Withdrawal symptoms can vary widely in severity, but generally include headaches, nausea, anxiety, fatigue, inability to focus, and irritability.

Keep a Food/Mood Diary

Keeping a food and mood diary or journal is one of the simplest biofeedback, self-help tools available.

First, numerous studies suggest that people who keep diaries manage to heal themselves on more than just psychological levels.

Many stress coaches encourage their clients to think of themselves as athletes. If you were a professional athlete, you would know whether you ran better in Nikes or Reeboks, whether your best times came after you ate steak and eggs for breakfast or porridge.

Keeping a diary helps you to both reinforce the behaviors that make you feel better and tune in to what makes you feel bad. This in turn encourages you to tune in to the higher intelligence of your body.

Call to Action

Opt for a natural high. Consider replacing caffeine, alcohol, nicotine and other stimulants with fresh juices, exercise, meditation, or some other activity which makes you feel great and sustains energy.

Coffee, tea, fizzy drinks, and other caffeinated beverages all have a diuretic effect, dehydrating the body. Herbal teas are healthy, caffeine-free alternatives. Try to drink 6-8 glasses (1.7-2 liters) of water a day to boost energy and flush out toxins.

18

STRESS-BUSTING FOODS

"The best six doctors anywhere—and no one can deny it - are sunshine, water, rest, and air, exercise and diet. These six will gladly you attend if only you are willing; Your mind they'll ease, your will they'll mend, and charge you not a shilling."

~ Nursery rhyme quoted by Wayne Fields, professor and writer

IT's easy to miss meals when you're busy, so plan for and opt for healthy snacks such as fruit, brown pitta bread with hummus and vegetable sticks with cubes of cheese, rather than crisps and chocolate.

Listed below are some helpful stress-busting food tips:

- Eat small but regular meals to sustain energy levels and keep blood sugar levels steady
- Shellfish, particularly oysters, are the richest source of zinc

- Complex carbohydrate foods, whole meal bread, pasta, wholegrain cereals and brown rice restore depleted energy levels
- Meat and fish contain beneficial amounts of iron, as do green leafy vegetables, dried apricots, lentils and other pulses
- Make sure you get sufficient amounts of B-group vitamins, particularly riboflavin, which converts carbohydrates into energy; vitamin B6 essential for energy metabolism; and vitamin B12, required for forming red blood cells that carry oxygen throughout the body. Useful sources of B-group vitamins include wholegrains, chicken, fish, eggs, dairy produce, pulses, shellfish and red meat
- Help your body absorb more iron by drinking a glass of orange juice once a day with a meal. Vitamin C also helps to boost energy
- Other vital minerals include magnesium, which works with potassium and sodium to ensure the efficient working of muscles, along with zinc, which protects against viral infections that often precede chronic fatigue
- Water plays a vital role in maintaining good health but few of us drink enough. It delivers nutrients around the body, regulates body temperature and transports waste. It is best to choose filtered or natural mineral water to achieve the desired daily amount. Coffee, tea and fizzy drinks contain caffeine, which has a diuretic effect, so they actually dehydrate the body. Herbal teas are healthy, caffeine-free alternatives. Try to drink 6-8 glasses (1.7-2 liters) of water a day

Avoid

- Avoid short-term energy boosters like caffeine, alcohol, and nicotine
- Avoid sugary foods, including biscuits, cakes, and chocolate. These also promote short term energy highs, leading to irritability and lethargy
- Alcohol in large quantities is draining on body and mind – although the occasional glass of wine can revive energy levels
- Refined carbohydrates foods like white bread, pasta and rice destabilize energy levels by causing a sharp increase in blood sugar levels

19

YOU BOOZE, YOU LOSE

"Drinking worked in the beginning: I felt wonderful, warm, and fuzzy. . .almost pretty. . .What I didn't know was that I was in a prison of my own making."

~ Colette Baron-Reid, intuitive & author

ALCOHOL AND STRESS don't make good marriage partners, but they're often fatally attracted.

Experience may have already taught you that too much booze muddles the mind, ignites aggression, reduces responsiveness, and ultimately depresses.

It's also hard to quit.

Alcohol—in large quantities it's draining on your body and mind —although the occasional glass of wine can revive energy levels. While you don't need to be a teetotaler, alcohol control will make you a better, healthier person.

Alcohol is a well-documented neurotoxin—a toxic substance that inhibits, damages, and destroys the tissues of your nervous system, especially your neurons (the conducting cells of your body's central nervous system).

Many successful people limit their drinking or consciously decide not to touch a drop. Keeping their resolve often takes extraordinary willpower.

"I spent last weekend suffering from a hangover after too many drinks on Friday night. It literally wiped my weekend and I didn't get any writing done," shares Joanna Penn on one of her blogs.

"I like a glass of wine but I'm not very good on it, and I was very angry with myself for going too far. I have a lot to do at the moment, so I need that time. For me, drinking alcohol does not serve my writing."

Author and public speaker Deepak Chopra gave up drinking. "I liked it too much," he once said. Steven King, after almost losing his family and destroying his writing career, managed to quit.

Other creatives like Amy Winehouse devastatingly never made it. At only 27, she died of alcohol poisoning on July 23, 2011. The risk of suicide also increases for stressed workers who turn to drink. As I've already discussed, alcohol abuse and excessive drinking is a major cause of anxiety and depression, impairs mental reasoning and critical thinking - increasing the likelihood of making tragic and often impulsive choices.

Risking destroying your career, ruining your relationships, sacrificing your sanity, and in the extreme, taking your life, is a massive price to pay for a mistaken belief that to cope with stress you must drink.

The many benefits of reducing your alcohol intake, or not drinking at all, include:

✓ A stronger ability to focus on your goals and dreams
✓ Improved confidence and self-esteem
✓ Increased productivity
✓ Increased memory, mental performance and decision-making
✓ Better control of your emotions

✓ Sweeter relationships
✓ Greater intuition and spiritual intelligence
✓ Authentic happiness

IF YOU'VE TRIED REDUCING the amount of alcohol you drink and have found it difficult, you're not alone. Not only do many people imbibe more booze in a frantic effort to reduce stress, but they underestimate how alcohol is highly addictive.

Not everyone has a battle with booze. Whether you cut back or eliminate alcohol entirely, the choice is ultimately yours. Only you know the benefits alcohol deliver or the success it destroys.

As one advance reader wrote to me:

> "I'm emailing you to let you know the impact your book has had on me. I cold-turkey stopped imbibing alcohol and coke and I've gained twenty years in energy. We all know we don't drink a lot, but what an insidious thing nightly alcohol is. Thank you for your book; its become a bit of a bible, or should I say they've become bits of bibles."

I'M SO PLEASED to know this! It's amazing how much productivity is gained by making changes to our health habits.

CALL TO ACTION

Would you like to reduce your alcohol consumption?

Try a period of sobriety. Experiment with living an alcohol-free life.

You'll find some sophisticated booze-free recipes in my book, *Mind Over Mojitos: How Moderating Your Drinking Can Change Your Life*. Scroll to the end of this book for your FREE excerpt

BE the first to know when my new book, *Mind Your Drink: The Surprising Joy of Being Sober* is released. I invite you to sign up for my newsletter.

20

ELIMINATE NEGATIVE EMOTIONS

"Keeping baggage from the past will leave no room for happiness in the future."

~ Wayne Misner

STRESS OVERLOAD CAN FLOOD your mind with negative emotions such as anxiety, depression, anger and resentment. Toxic emotions, if left unresolved, are insidious thieves of energy and vitality.

Avoid Groundhog Day. Don't let people, things, or situations which trigger unhealed wounds or that spark irritability take you prisoner. Pinpoint the causes and look for solutions.

Resist the urge to play "victim." In the short term it may seem like the easy option, but long term, this unresolved source of stress will create havoc on your mind, body, and soul.

Anger prepares your body to fight, and it does a lot of damage to your brain and body if you're in a situation where you sustain those stress chemicals. The Thymus gland begins to shrivel up and this can make you susceptible to internal organ ulceration.

Anger can even kill you – you could have an aneurism or heart blockage. Furthermore, when you trigger the stress response by getting angry, it effectively disengages the thinking part of the brain, the cerebral cortex – which is fine if you need to launch into combat. Though it doesn't help if you need to choose the best response, to stop and muse on the merits of your chosen course of action.

There is incredibly wide-spread ignorance of how emotions actually work. People struggle with the idea that we can actually choose our emotions. It is impossible for anyone to make another person angry, sad, depressed, or happy - without their consent. There is always a point of choice - no matter how fleeting this decisive moment may seem.

Endorphin's – the brain's own morphine

Endorphins are the brain's own opiates - they decrease stress and promote feelings of happiness. They also aid sleep.

There are lots of activities and stimuli that can promote the release of endorphins and therefore inhibit the stress response and offset negative emotions; for example, exercise (the runner's high), sexual activity, certain kinds of music (especially those that cause a tingle up your spine), and doing something you feel passionate about.

Some "feel good" foods also increase endorphin levels. We'll explore some of these mood foods later in this book.

CALL TO ACTION

If you're struggling to deal with negative emotions there's a wealth of help on hand. Self-help your way to success; talk to a supportive, wise friend, or seek advice from a counselor, psychologist, life coach, or other expert. Remember, "a problem shared is a problem solved."

Consider reading my Millionaire Mindset book. Even though it was written for authors, the strategies apply to anyone who wants to overcome negative emotions and develop more empowering beliefs.

21

MEMORIES – UNSTICKING THOSE THAT STICK

"I told my audience that if they changed their beliefs they could change their lives. It was a familiar conclusion with familiar responses from participants: 'Well Bruce, that's great, but how do we do that?'"

~ Bruce Lipton, developmental biologist

STRESSFUL or emotionally intense experiences stimulate hormones that activate parts of the brain associated with housing memories and emotions. The secretion of epinephrine (adrenaline) and cortisol stimulate the amygdala.

The amygdala in turn stimulates the hippocampus and the cerebral cortex, which are both important for memory storage. However, excessive or prolonged stress, with correspondingly prolonged cortisol, impairs memory.

This explains why people find it so difficult to forget traumatic and stressful events – often replaying them again and again in their minds. The emotional charge that the event held consolidates and strengthens the memory into long-term storage.

If the traumatic event is not processed and worked through, the emotional charge remains, locking it further in the cellular structure of the brain. Counseling or reprogramming using hypnosis are some of the many techniques that may be necessary to help you **change your view of the event.**

For example, one effective and powerful counseling technique used to assist people who are suffering from Post-Traumatic Stress Disorder is called "Rapid Eye Desensitization." It works by removing/altering the previous bio-chemical or structural change the trauma of the event created.

Whilst counseling and reframing techniques in general can help you to gain a new perspective, "Rapid Eye Desensitization" weakens the emotional charge.

SHIFTING Self-Limiting Beliefs

Traumatic memories leave a residue of unhelpful beliefs; yet so often, we aren't even aware of what our self-limiting beliefs are. If your unhelpful thoughts are ingrained, or you keep sabotaging your own success, seeking help from a qualified practitioner with expertise in reprogramming stubborn, disempowering beliefs may be a game-changer.

A wonderful counselor with whom I trained to be a Worklife Solutions Certified Life Coach recommended the book *The Biology of Belief: Unleashing the Power of Consciousness, Matter & Miracles*, by Bruce Lipton.

Lipton is an American developmental biologist best known for promoting the idea that genes and DNA can be manipulated by a person's beliefs.

In his book, he shares how he experienced a paradigm shift while at a conference. Back then, Lipton, like so many of us, didn't fully realize the crucial role the subconscious mind plays in the change process.

"Instead, I relied mostly on trying to power through negative behavior, using positive thinking and willpower. I knew, though, that I had had only limited success in making personal changes in my own life.

"I also knew that when I offered this solution, the energy in the room dropped like a lead balloon. It seems my sophisticated audiences had already tried willpower and positive thinking with limited success."

Fate intervened for Lipton, as it did for me when I was guided to his book. So often life whispers to us, but we fail to tune in. In Lipton's case, the messenger he needed to hear was sitting right next to him; psychotherapist Rob Williams, the creator of the self-help tool PSYCH-K, was presenting at the same conference.

"Rob's opening remarks quickly had the entire audience on the edge of our seats. In his introduction, Rob stated that PSYCH-K can change long-standing, limiting beliefs in a matter of minutes," Lipton wrote.

In his book *The Biology of Belief*, Lipton shares how, in less than 10 minutes, a woman paralyzed by her fear of public speaking transformed into a confident, excited, and visibly relaxed person up on the stage. The transformation Lipton witnessed was so astounding, he has since used PYSCH-K in his own life.

"PSYCH-K has helped me undo my self-limiting beliefs, including one about not being able to finish my book," Lipton wrote at the end of his book.

That struck a chord with me. I felt a trill of excitement. Not a thrill, but a trill—a song deep in my heart. Lipton was like the Pied Piper and I was happy to follow. At the time, I had so many unfinished books and had published nothing.

A month after working with a PSYCH-K trained practitioner, I finished the first two books in my *Mid-Life Career Rescue* series. Soon after, I released my third, *Midlife Career Rescue: Employ Yourself*, followed quickly by a fourth book, *How to Find Your Passion and Purpose*.

At the time of writing, I have also published three romance books under my pen name, Mollie Mathews.

Now, you're reading my fourteenth book—all completed within the last two years. All because, despite feeling skeptical (and a little vulnerable), I sought help to reprogram my mindset.

CALL TO ACTION

If traumatic memories or unhelpful beliefs are ingrained, or you keep sabotaging your own success, seeking help from a qualified practitioner with expertise in reprogramming stubborn, disempowering beliefs may be a game-changer.

Chances are you don't need to see a therapist to move beyond self-limiting beliefs; but if you do, go and get help. There's magic in that.

You can also learn from some of the most powerful, effective, and simple techniques used by practitioners working in the realm of positive psychology and mind reprogramming. This includes hypnosis—something you'll discover in the next chapter.

22

HYPNOTIZE YOUR MILLIONAIRE MIND

"Hypnosis is the epitome of mind-body medicine. It can enable the
mind to tell the body how to react and modify the messages that
the body sends to the mind."

~ *New York Times*

To GET the tremendous power of your unconscious mind behind
your goals, you will need to program it for success. A simple and
exceedingly effective way to do this is through hypnosis.

"Emotional problems work much more on the 'feeling level' than
the 'thinking level' which is why just trying to think differently is so
hard," say the UK-based hypnotherapists at Uncommon Knowledge.

"We use hypnosis to help you feel different quickly which then
makes you think differently about a situation."

You can access hypnosis sessions from the comfort of your home
via instant download. But a word of caution first—the Internet is
awash with websites which offer hypnosis products and services that
have not been created by experienced and qualified professionals.

Some of these programs are of limited or no use, while others may do more harm than good.

One of my favourite hypnosis sites is run by the UK-based company Uncommon Knowledge. On their website, www.hypnosisdownloads.com, you'll find a range of self-hypnosis mp3 audios, including *The Millionaire Mindset* program. In their own words, they confirm that the program contains the following six success-shaping sessions:

1) Create Winning Business Ideas—enter a creative space within your mind where the money-making ideas will flow like molten gold.

2) Create Real Business Passion—generate a powerful deep unconscious drive for your business idea that will propel you forward.

3) Build Unshakeable Self-Belief—every successful entrepreneur has solid self-confidence and self-belief. Build yours so you can beat the nay-sayers and weather the storms with ease.

4) Generate Laser Focus—you don't get to the top by drifting off and thinking about other things. Get the full power of your unconscious mind behind your goals.

5) Develop an Unstoppable Work Ethic—anyone who tells you becoming a millionaire is not hard work has never done it. This session will make work your most enjoyable pastime.

6) Create Unbeatable Optimism—as you travel your business path, you will come up against obstacles. There will be times when you wonder if you should give up. This session will give you a solid bedrock of optimism, so you just know it's going to work, even on the darkest of days.

UK based hypnotherapist Marissa Peer says that there are only three things you need to know about your mind: it likes what is familiar, it responds to the pictures in your head, and it gravitates to what you desire. Harness the power of your mind to create prosperous productivity by intensifying your desire, visualizing success, and making productivity part of your daily ritual.

Along with hypnosis, creating a productivity vision board, saying daily affirmations, and writing at a regular time are just some of the many ways you can apply these three mind tools.

CALL TO ACTION

Research the benefits of hypnosis.

Experiment with this powerful technique.

Program your subconscious mind for prosperous productivity.

23

RATIONAL EMOTIVE BEHAVIORAL THERAPY

"The primary cause of unhappiness is not the situation, but your thoughts about it. Be aware of the thoughts you are thinking. Separate them from the situation, which is always neutral, which always is as it is."

~ Eckhart Tolle

ALBERT ELLIS's Rational Emotive Behaviour Therapy (REBT) origi- nated in the mid 1950's as he became increasingly aware of the inef- fectiveness of psychoanalysis to produce change in his patients.

The REBT worldview is that people often make themselves emotional victims by their own distorted, unrealistic, and irrational thinking patterns. Ellis takes an essentially optimistic view of people, but criticizes some humanistic approaches as being too soft at times and failing to address the fact that people can virtually "self-destruct" through irrational and muddled thinking.

According to Ellis and the REBT worldview, all people are born with self-defeating tendencies. When something goes against your goals, your values or desires, feelings of failure, rejection, etc., can set in; but you have a choice.

You have a choice of feeling terrified, panicky, depressed, self-pitying, self-doubting, etc. —and succumbing to these emotions. But these feelings can prevent you from making positive changes. Which emotion you choose, according to REBT practitioners, is thought to mainly depend on your belief system—not your goals and values, but what you tell yourself when your goals and values are thwarted or blocked.

We all have a rational set of beliefs called "preferences." In this context, "rational" means self-helping beliefs, such as, "I don't like what is going on." "I wish it weren't so." "How annoying." "Let's see what I can do about it."

Many people very frequently pick irrational beliefs, referred to as "demands," such as, "Because I don't like what is going on, it absolutely should not be allowed." "It can't happen." "I can't stand it." "Everyone should love me – if they don't, I am worthless." "It's horrible, I think I'll give up" (or, when taken to the extreme, "I'll kill myself").

Ellis' therapeutic approach is not to challenge the clients' goals and values, but instead *attack* their absolute demands about achieving these values. The emphasis of the therapy is on changing the way the client thinks about the behavior or the upsetting event, rather than on changing the behavior itself.

This is a critical point—it is not the actual event but our view of the event that is critical.

The task of the REBT therapist is to correct clients' thought patterns and minimize irrational ideas, while simultaneously helping them to change their dysfunctional feelings and behaviors. Challenging the irrational statement is key to changing an entire philosophy of life.

The ABCDEF Method

PERHAPS ELLIS'S most important concrete methodological contribution is his A-B-C–D-E-F theory, which can be summarized as follows:

A - the "objective" facts, events, behaviors that an individual encounters

B - the person's beliefs about 'A'

C - the emotional consequences, or how a person feels and acts about 'A'

D - disputing 'B' irrational beliefs

E - effect that disputation has on the client

F - new feelings and behaviors

EXAMPLE:

1. John's organization has just announced a restructure. There is a lack of communication about the changes

2. John believes the restructure is a waste of time and that his employer is being deliberately secretive. He thinks they should leave everything the same so he could get on with his job.

3. He feels angry, depressed and resentful.

4. John challenges his belief that the restructure is a waste of time. He realizes that changes outside the organization mean that they must change or risk losing their market share. This would mean he could lose his job. He thinks his bosses are probably still working out what they need to do and that when they are ready they will let him know

5. This change in thinking affects John by making him consider alternatives that his mind had been closed to before.

6. John feels calmer, and more optimistic. He decides to take control by asking questions about the changes, and

seeking the services of a career coach to help him prepare for opportunities both externally and internally.

CALL TO ACTION: **Your A-B-C–D-E-F Strategy**

Consider applying this technique to a current or past stressful situation.

24

MEDITATE

"Our brains never get a break and the results can be increased stress, anxiety, insomnia and, if left unchecked, even depression. But there is something you can do—nothing."

~ Mathew Johnstone, author & cartoonist

STRESSED, fatigued, or overwhelmed minds will never be productive. The opposite is also true—peaceful, calm, and clear minds elevate success.

Many of the most influential authors, creative artists, and business people today credit their meditative practice for their increased productivity and prosperity.

"It's the Swiss army knife of medical tools, for conditions both small and large," writes Arianna Huffington, the founder of *The Huffington Post* and author of *Thrive*.

When Tim Ferriss, who practices transcendental meditation, sat down with more than 200 people at the height of their field for his new book, *Tools of Titans*, he found that 80% followed some form of guided mindfulness practice.

It took Ferriss a while to get into meditation, he says in a podcast episode about his own morning routine. But since he discovered that the majority of world-class performers meditated, he also decided to follow the habit.

His practice takes up 21 minutes a day: one minute to get settled and 20 minutes to meditate.

Ferriss recommends two apps for those wanting some help getting started—*Headspace* or *Calm*.

"Start small, rig the game so you can win it, get in five sessions before you get too ambitious with length," says Ferriss.

"You have to win those early sessions so you establish it as a habit, so you don't have the cognitive fatigue of that practice."

So, what's the buzz? Here are a few of the many ways a regular meditative practice will improve your productivity:

- Decreased stress and anxiety
- Improved focus, memory, and learning ability
- Fantastic recharging capacity
- Higher IQ and more efficient brain functioning
- Increased blood circulation and reduced hyperactivity in the brain, slower wavelengths and decreased beta waves (Beta State:13—30Hz) means more time between thoughts which leads to more skillful decision making
- Increased Theta State (4—8Hz) and Delta States (1—3 Hz) which deepens awareness and strengthens intuition and visualization skills
- Increased creativity and connection with your higher intelligence

RECENT RESEARCH PUBLISHED in *New Scientist* has revealed that meditation can help to calm people and reduce fear. The research found that regular meditation can tame the amygdala, an area of the brain which is the hub of fear memory.

People who meditate regularly are less likely to be shocked, flustered, surprised, or as angry as other people, and have a greater stress tolerance threshold as a result.

By meditating regularly, the brain is reoriented from a stressful fight-or-flight response to one of acceptance, a shift that increases contentment, enthusiasm, and feelings of happiness.

"I started meditating, and I do it twice a day. It's kind of like anything that you—it's just about being quiet, like drawing back on the reins and it allows me to have energy." – Hugh Jackman

CALL TO ACTION

Many successful people regularly take time to focus on the present moment. Make meditating for at least 20 minutes a day part of your daily routine for optimum success and well-being.

Consistency is key. Shorter meditations on a regular basis are more productive than long sessions every few weeks. If you are a beginner, you may prefer to aim for 5 minutes a day and add 1 minute each week.

Many people find that meditating for 20 minutes in the morning and 20 minutes at the end of the day yields remarkable benefits.

25

PRAYER THERAPY

"Prayer is when you talk to God; Meditation is when you listen to God."

~ Diana Robinson, author

HARNESS THE ENERGIES of love and boost your purposeful productivity and tenacity to succeed with the sacred daily ritual of prayer.

If prayer is something you are unfamiliar with or hold negative associations about, don't be deterred. Whatever your experience or belief system, prayer is simply a form of spiritual communion. It's a very simple and potent tool used successfully by many prosperous people.

Many people have lost their union with God because of the hypocritical dogma which has polluted many faith systems. However, you will discover in this chapter that prayer comes in many shapes, colors, and textures.

As the author of *The Alchemist*, Paulo Coelho, shares on the back jacket of his book, *The Spy* (a fascinating story about Mata Hari),

Coelho has "Experimented with magic and alchemy, studied philosophy and religion, read voraciously, lost and recovered his faith, and experienced the pain and pleasure of love.

"In searching for his own place in the world, he has discovered answers for the challenges that everybody faces. He believes that within ourselves, we have the necessary strength to find our destiny."

One of the key tools that has given him strength is prayer. As he writes in the foreword to *The Spy,* "O Mary, conceived without sin, pray for us who have recourse to You. Amen."

Many prosperous creatives and successful business people, including Coco Chanel, Julia Cameron, Wayne Dyer and Louise Hay, refer to prayer in several forms, including describing it as the voice of God, intuition, higher self, inner goddess, or their Sacred Divine.

In her book *Illuminata: A Return to Prayer,* Marianne Williamson speaks of prayer as a way of "focusing our eyes," dramatically transforming our orientation, releasing us "from the snares of lower energies," and aligning "our internal energies with truth."

In their book *The Energies of Love,* intuitive healer Donna Eden and psychiatrist David Feinstein refer to the action of prayer as inviting an inspiring invocation.

Dictionary.com refers to an invocation as the "act of invoking or calling upon a deity, spirit, etc., for aid, protection, inspiration, or the like." The website also defines invocation as "an entreaty for aid and guidance from a Muse."

Saying a simple prayer "alerts your sensibilities to dimensions that your senses do not perceive," say Eden and Feinstein.

In their book, they share how they are not consistent with their use of invocations, but use them most when they are about to embark on anything creative.

"Dozens of mini-prayers have infused the writing of this book, sometimes asking for wisdom, clarity, focus, and humor; other times asking that you, dear reader, receive guidance that gives your relationship greater ease, depth, healing, and joy."

Below are a few examples of their collective and individual invocations:

We ask that we touch people deeply and in ways that enhance their spirits, well-being, and mastery of their energies.

I ask this day for opportunities to love, to flourish, and to heal that which thirsts for healing.

I ask for support so that which is purest within me can shine through me.

Acting on the recommendation in their book to create my own invocation by referring to the writings of Rumi, one of my favorite poetic mystics, I wrote the below invocation from which I draw sustenance and purpose (my adaption appears in parentheses):

I have one small drop of knowing in my soul. (Fill my heart with wisdom and) let it dissolve in your ocean (spreading healing waves of comfort, hope, and joy to all those who bathe in the waters of our words).

Scientific (4-step) prayer therapy is another form of invoking guidance and "the only real answer to the great deception," writes Joseph Murphy (PhD.) in his excellent book, *The Miracle of Mind Dynamics*. "Let the light of God shine in your mind, and you will neutralize the harmful effects of the negatives implanted in your subconscious mind."

The four steps Murphy suggests are:

- Recognition of the healing presence of Infinite Intelligence
- Complete acceptance of the One Power
- Affirmation of the Truth
- Rejoice and give thanks for the answer

"Faith is action in love," Mother Theresa once said. Whatever mode of prayer or invocation you use, read them slowly and deliberately and notice how the energies in your mind, body and soul shift.

The indicator of God's presence in you is the presence of peace, harmony, abundance, and joy.

CALL TO ACTION

Develop your own invocations and prayers, or refer to helpful books such as: *lluminata: A Return to Prayer* by Marianne Williamson; *Prayers to the Great Creator* by Julia Cameron; or collections by the Persian mystic and poet Rumi and the artist and poet Kahil Gibran.

Embark on scientific prayer therapy.

Take the time to stop and pray from your heart. The words that you use aren't as important compared to the strength of your desire to connect with The Divine.

Be open to a response appearing which is different from your expectations—and know that your prayers are heard and answered.

26

JOURNAL YOUR WAY TO SUCCESS

"I love my writing journal. It's my partner in writing, there for me whenever I need it, my confidant and my supporter and my record of where I've been."

~ Anne Gracie, romance author

RECENTLY, while tackling a mammoth writing project, I talked myself into a bit of a funk. I knew that what I really needed were some positive reminders of my intentions. Instead of saying "I quit" and "I am so over this," and retelling the story that allowed for failure, I went online and purchased a beautiful black sketchbook.

Prior to this, I had noticed anxiety building—as it always does when I don't have a special book in which to purge and reshape my thoughts.

With my gold pen, I wrote some of the most empowering and encouraging quotes from other authors who have also struggled to maintain a prosperous mindset while writing an epic book.

Top of my list was Jessie Burton's empowering words, "Always picture succeeding, never let it fade. Always picture success, no matter how badly things seem to be going in the moment."

These words reminded me that I was picturing failure. I was telling myself messages of failure. I was feeling failure.

Jesse Burton, the author of *The Muse and The Miniaturist*, is very inspiring to me because she is so honest about her own battles with mental health—including anxiety.

"In February, I was publicly honest about how difficult it had been to handle, process and assimilate in real time some of the changes in my life. Namely, the strange and wondrous effects of *The Miniaturist*. I wrote about anxiety, my first tentative foray into putting that mental morass into words," she wrote in one of her newsletters.

As Burton highlights, blogging and sharing your thoughts with your fans is another form of cathartic journaling—as is writing a book like this.

"You could have talked more about your personal experience so that other writers can more easily relate to you," wrote an advance reader of this book.

You'll notice in this chapter and throughout this book that I've woven in more of my experiences, the highs and the lows, as a result.

To minimize stress and boost your success mindset, another form of journaling is writing Morning Pages, a strategy developed by Julia Cameron, author of *The Artist's Way*.

The writing is just a stream of consciousness, writing out what-ever you are feeling—good (or what one of my clients calls the "sun-nies") or not so good ("the uglies").

"It's a way of clearing the mind—a farewell to what has been and a hello to what will be," Cameron says.

"Write down just what is crossing your consciousness. Cloud thoughts that move across consciousness. Meeting your shadow and taking it out for a cup of coffee so it doesn't eddy your consciousness during the day."

The point of this writing is to work with your subconscious and let it work its magic in the creative, healing process.

CALL TO ACTION

Keep a writing journal for specific writing projects. It may not work for you, but you will never know until you try.

Start where you are—commit to a daily practice of writing Morning Pages and journal for self-exploration.

DIVE DEEPER...

If you would love to explore the idea of employing yourself and creating a passion and purpose inspired business, *The Passion-Driven Business Planning Journal: The Effortless Path to Manifesting Your Business and Career Goals*, will help. Available as a paperback and eBbook—navigate to here viewBook.at/PassionBusinessJournal

OR YOU MAY PREFER to take my online course, and watch inspirational and practical videos and other strategies to help you to fulfil your potential—https://the-coaching-lab.teachable.com/p/follow-your-passion-and-purpose-to-prosperity.

YOU CAN FIND out more about Morning Pages here http://juliacameronlive.com/basic-tools/morning-pages/

27

CONSULT THE ORACLES

"Faith in the guidance of Spirit gives you the courage to take risks because you're assured that whatever happens, a Higher Power is on your side and you will survive."

~ Colette Baron-Reid, intuitive & author

IT MAY SURPRISE you to know that many Titans consult oracles to improve their mindset and boost their productivity and performance.

Subjects such as astrology, psychic phenomena, spirituality, and a fascination with tarot and oracle cards have helped many creative people and successful entrepreneurs overcome doubt, strengthen their beliefs, clarify their direction and find meaning in challenging situations.

As I discussed earlier, I've experienced incredible benefits, both in terms of renewed clarity and confidence and in boosting my productivity, by making consulting oracles part of my morning ritual.

My first experience with psychic phenomena and the Tarot was when I was a teenager in New Zealand in the late 70s. Like for Coco Chanel, it's a fascination that stayed with me throughout my life and which continues to provide inspiration, courage, and fortitude—both personally and professionally.

My daughter, Hannah, is also a gifted intuitive and offers angel card readings professionally via her business, Co-Creators of Joy.

"Increasing numbers of people are looking to ancient oracles to receive personal guidance because they are not getting the answers and insights they need when they consult the usual sources of psychology and science," says intuitive counselor Colette Baron-Reid.

However, there are some highly influential psychologists who honor the wisdom and intuitive guidance that oracles herald.

Of all the psychological theories in the West, that of revered Swiss psychologist Carl Jung stands out as most applicable to Tarot.

Jung wrote about Tarot on several occasions, seeing it as depicting archetypes of transformation like those he found in myths, dreams, and alchemy.

He described its divinatory abilities as similar to the ancient divination text I Ching and to astrology, and later in life established a group which attempted to integrate insights about a person based on multiple divination systems including Tarot.

Applying Oracles to Your Day

"The Greeks believed our genius was not part of us but was a divine visitation. Our jobs, as artists and writers, was to become the best possible vessel for that genius. Part of that is to be forever learning, improving, expanding, and experimenting," writes Jessa Crispin in her fabulous book, *The Creative Tarot: A Modern Guide to an Inspired Life.*

In her book, Crispin discusses the origin of the Tarot and how the creator of *The Rider-Waite Tarot Deck*, A.E. Waite, believed the purpose of the cards was for elevating the soul and making what is unconscious, conscious. Like many other mystics, Waite, also a scholar with ties to both the Golden Dawn and the Freemasons, believed there was a divine order; he believed our role as creatives was to align ourselves with Universal consciousness and become a conduit or channel for its wisdom, like the Magician in the Tarot.

A simple and truly awe-inspiringly powerful way Jessa Crispin, Isabel Allende, and other authors learn, improve, expand, and grow is by applying oracles to their daily writing. They may do this by drawing a card to help with focus or well-being or by using the cards to guide the creation of their story.

At the time of writing this chapter, I asked for guidance and drew a card at random from *The Rider-Waite Tarot Deck*. This is the deck recommended in Jessa Crispin's book, *The Creative Tarot*.

The card I drew was "Knight of Pentacles." I smiled when I saw the image on the front of the card—a knight siting on a horse. The horse faces right, like the image on my cover. And I dedicate many of my self-empowerment books to my partner, whom I refer to as my Templar Knight.

Instantly, I felt a surge of joyful connection. The message Crispin provides in her book, which I found most relevant as guidance, is provided below. It was extremely relevant to me today. I'm sure it will speak to you:

Knight of Pentacles

The Knight of Coins is slow to get moving, but once he does, he is unstoppable. He is the Knight of the Crusades—in it for the long haul and also for the plunder. He is grounded, cautious enough to know how not to storm into a predicament that might get him killed, but also dedicated. He wins by outlasting you, by grinding you down slowly.

...but to have the strength to endure a long battle. A city does not fall in a day. Make sure that you're going to be able to stick it out.

...When you draw the Knight of Coins, you need to ask: How is your body engaged with this project? Does how you feel about your own body transmit into the work? Do you take care of your body so that you have the stamina to stay committed to a long-term project, or are you on a Gummi-Bear-and-iced-coffee sugar high? Because the Knight of Coins believes in doing the work, in showing up every day until the job is done—and for that, one needs to keep the body as strong as the mind.

This card reminded me of several things. Firstly, that even when I can't see the results of my intentions, I must continue to trust Spirit, the magnetism of writing, and the importance of creating with passion.

As Dame Anita Roddick, founder of the organic skincare company The Body Shop once said, "We create with passion and passion sells."

Secondly, and importantly, the message about tuning into my body barometer reminds me to protect my health and ensure that what I feed my mind, body, and soul increases, not strips, my stamina, fortitude, and resilience.

As Hal Enrod writes in *The Miracle Morning for Writer's*, "As a writer, it's important to manage your energy level. The craft we've chosen is amazing, but it's also one of the most sedentary ways to spend your time...We all know it's important to exercise, read, and eat healthy foods because these habits will have a significant long-term impact on your life, but they are often put on the back burner."

Your health truly is your wealth, as I share in the next section.

CALL TO ACTION

Experiment with Tarot—either have a reading with an experienced Tarot card reader or study the cards and their meanings for yourself.

I highly recommend going online and purchasing a copy of *The Rider-Waite Tarot Deck* and Jessa Crispin's book, *The Creative Tarot: A Modern Guide to an Inspired Life,* and making these tools part of your daily writing ritual.

Feed your curiosity—take note of the places and circumstances where Tarot, astrological symbols, and other mystical and occultist philosophies are used—in business and life.

28

MAINTAIN SOME BALANCE

"Every now and then go away, have a little relaxation, for when you
come back to your work your judgment will be surer. Go some
distance away because then the work appears smaller and more of
it can be taken in at a glance and a lack of harmony and
proportion is more readily seen."

~ Leonardo da Vinci

WORKAHOLISM IS an addiction for many passionate people. Others
use overwork to medicate their unhappiness in other areas of their
life—most commonly dissatisfaction with their relationships.

When you work slavishly, particularly at something you love,
your brain releases chemicals called opiates which create feelings of
euphoria. No wonder it's hard to step away!

Euphoria stems from the Greek word *euphoría*—the power of
enduring easily. But consider what the state of endurance implies.
Enduring implies force or strain, or gritting your teeth and bearing it
at times. Force or strain with no respite leads to stress, overload, and

burnout—robbing you of vital energy and depleting your millionaire mindset.

Many people find when they don't step away from their work they suffer disillusionment, and things that once filled them with passion, including their current writing projects, no longer fills them with joy. Resentment builds and relationships with family, friends, and colleagues can also suffer.

Working addictively offers a short-term fix, but lasting happiness needs variety and nourishment. Being with family or friends, engaging in a hobby, spending time in nature, learning something new, helping others, or just being solitary will help you avoid burnout, nourish your brain, heart, and soul, improve your judgment, and restore harmony.

To be truly happy and successful, you must be able to be at peace when you are working and when you are at rest.

Leonardo da Vinci would often take breaks from his work to refresh his mind and spirit. While others claimed that he took too long to finish things, he knew the importance of replenishing his focus to maintain a clear perspective.

Here we are still talking about him over 500 years later.

Leonardo also valued sleep, noting in one of his journals that some of his best insights came when his mind was not working.

Even if you love the work that you do, and think your book is the greatest thing since man launched into space, it's fun to get away from it and have objective-free time to unwind and reset.

When you return to your work, your focus will be surer, your vision refreshed, and your confidence bolder.

CALL TO ACTION

Who are you when you are not working? Do you still feel successful? Do you feel worthy?

When was the last time you truly relaxed? Can you think of a time when you stepped away from your work and when you returned, your mind was clearer, your confidence surer?

Schedule time out—and be firm with yourself. Stay away from anything that feeds your addiction.

What can you start doing, stop doing, do more or less of? What benefits will flow from these changes?

29

REST

"Happiness is a butterfly, which when pursued, is always beyond your grasp, but which, if you will sit down quietly may alight upon you."

~ Nathaniel Hawthorne, author

WHEN YOUR STRESS levels are high and you get depressed, angry, tense, and lethargic or begin to experience tension headaches etc., that should be a very simple biofeedback signal that you are better off stopping, re-evaluating your choices and taking some time out.

Sometimes this can be easier said than done. In our overachiever, overstimulated society, where many people spend more hours every week with their eyes riveted to their iPhone, instead of spending quality time on their own or with family and friends, the whole concept of stopping and resting to restore ourselves is almost unusual. But resting to replenish is essential to well-being.

We're pushing ourselves all day long with energy that we don't have. The most common complaint people go to the doctor for is fatigue. Research conducted by a company helping people suffering from adrenal fatigue claims that 80% of people don't have as much energy as they'd like to have.

"It's because we're pushing and using caffeine, sugar and energy drinks and nicotine and stress for energy rather than running on our own energy."

Long-term stress and long-term cortisol will literally alter a person's hormonal profile.

Rest allows the adrenal glands to restore, enabling cortisol levels to return to normal. Long-term stress and long-term cortisol overload can lead to adrenal fatigue and burn-out, altering your hormonal profile, and making it more difficult to return to the real, inspired, happy and creative you.

CALL TO ACTION

Give yourself permission to take time every day and every week to have fun, rest your mind and rest your body.

"You're getting pretty good
at this stress management thing."

30

SLEEP

"By helping us keep the world in perspective, sleep gives us a chance to refocus on the essence of who we are. And in that place of connection, it is easier for the fears and concerns of the world to drop away."

~ Arianna Huffington, businesswoman

TIME STAYS LONG ENOUGH for those who use it well and protect it fiercely. But many people either find it difficult to switch off at night, or they sacrifice their sleep in the mistaken belief they'll be more productive.

Sleep plays a vital role in your health and wellbeing. Getting enough quality sleep helps you maintain your mental and physical health and enhances your quality of life.

Modern science proves conclusively that if you skip out on sleep you're compromising not just your productivity and efficiency, but also your health.

More than a third of American adults are not getting enough

sleep on a regular basis, according to a February 2016 study from the Centers for Disease Control and Prevention.

Sleeping less than seven hours a day, they report, can lead to an increased risk of frequent mental distress, impaired thinking, reduced cognitive ability, and increased susceptibility to depression.

Lack of sleep also increases the likelihood of obesity, diabetes, high blood pressure, heart disease, and stroke. None of which will aid your quest for happiness and prosperity.

When stress becomes too much, is your quality of sleep affected? The next time you're worrying and feeling anxious around bedtime, try one of these simple hacks to relax and quieten your mind enough to fall asleep:

TAKE time to unwind after a stressful day

Before going to bed, take some time out to unwind from the stresses of the day. Allow at least 30 minutes before bed for a quiet, "preparing to sleep" activity. Enjoying a calming cup of herbal tea, listening to soothing music, reading a novel or book of poems (paperback), an aromatherapy bath with lavender and other scented oils, or even a relaxation or meditation practice.

CLEAR MENTAL CLUTTER

If you have the events of the day or other issues running through your head before bedtime, start writing them down in a journal for you to revisit later. The simple act of writing down your troubles – and noting how you feel about them in that moment – can help you make sense of the root cause of your problem and free up some space for more important activities like sleeping.

SCHEDULE TIME TO worry

If you want to sleep better, you need to empty your mind of all thoughts, tasks and stresses. Another way to clear your mental chatter is to "box your worries" by scheduling in dedicated "worry time." This is a programmed time that is dedicated to – you guessed it – worrying. A scheduled 30-minute window in your day allows you, and even encourages you, to think constructively through the problem. Many of my clients tell me that when their "worry time" comes around, their issue has disappeared or become less important.

If the worrying issue is still lingering, by granting yourself some time to focus it, you're forced to either formulate a solution, or to let it go.

BE proactive and create a to-do list

Another active way to clear your head and get to bed is with a master to-do list. Write down "things to do" in a list in your diary so that you don't need to keep thinking about them over and over. This is why planning your "tomorrow" the day before is also an effective strategy. You can sleep well knowing that you have your bases covered. This also minimizes decision fatigue.

Did you know that humans are only capable of keeping seven to nine different things in our working memories at once? When you try to recall all the tasks you need to complete, this uses up valuable mental energy and can prevent you from sleeping soundly.

Creating a list transfers your chores from your mind to the page (paper or digital), freeing up valuable brainpower. You'll be better able to analyze tasks and prioritize, delegate, or even eliminate some of them. It's a win-win success strategy.

Numerous studies reveal that a to-do list can also make you happier. Don't sweat it if you don't manage to cross everything off your list; the act of compiling one can still help you reach your goals, manage your stress levels, and help you relax enough to get some well-earned sleep time.

DISCONNECT

You can also enhance your sleep by turning off all devices and leaving them outside your bedroom.

"I will not sleep with my phone in my room," Jessie Burton, author of *The Muse*, shared on one of her blogs. After suffering from burnout and severe anxiety, she created a not-to-do list to restore and protect her mental health.

In the next chapter, you'll dive deeper and uncover the life-changing benefits of unplugging, taking control of technology, and enjoying regular digital detoxes.

CALL TO ACTION

If lack of sleep is keeping you awake and night and making you tired during the day, consider reading and applying the strategies in Arianna Huffington's book, *The Sleep Revolution: Transforming Your Life One Night at a Time.*

Be ruthless about prioritizing your well-being. Remind yourself of the benefits that flow while you sleep, and when you enhance the length and quality of your sleep.

31

UNPLUG

"Setting aside protected time each day for direct interaction with people—or for solitude and meditation without the interruption of a Facebook feed or a stream of texts—instinctively feels like a good thing."

~ John Swartzberg, M.D.

"WE'RE SUFFERING A SLEEP CRISIS," warns Arianna Huffington, co-founder and editor-in-chief of *The Huffington Post* and author of *The Sleep Revolution: Transforming Your Life One Night at a Time*. The chronic need to be "plugged in" is hurting our health, productivity, relationships, and happiness.

Are you suffering from information overwhelm? Are you permanently attached to your device? Does the thought of unplugging send your anxiety spiraling? What if you miss something? What if....what if...

What if you shut it all down and stepped away for a day, a week, a month, or more?

Consider taking time out to unplug, take a step back, forget about what is expected, forget about what you may be missing, and think about what you may be gaining.

Like with breaking any addiction, unplugging can be a struggle at first, but the benefits are worth it. Besides the main benefit of being able to enjoy much more hassle-free, uninterrupted time, here are seven other wonderful and lesser-known upsides you'll notice from making the decision to unplug regularly:

Increased awareness. When was the last time you were fully aware of the beauty that surrounds you? When you unplug, you blitz major distractions. You begin to notice small details in people, things, and places that you never really noticed before.

Clarity. Unplugging reduces brain overload. Technological over-stimulation overwhelms your mind, reducing your cognitive reasoning skills.

Improved memory retention and mood. Even just detoxing from technology for a day once a week is enough to give your brain a reboot, which can improve your memory and lift your mood.

More brain power. Spending less time being a slave to technological stimulation provides more time to focus on doing activities that can grow your brain cells—such as indulging in an enjoyable hobby, learning a new skill, visiting a new place, having new experiences, or going for a relaxing walk.

Enhanced relationships. Disconnecting from your perpetual tether to iPhones and laptops can do all kinds of great things for your real-world connections with families and friends. This is a no-brainer, but one so many people seem to miss. Putting your device away and giving the people you are with, rather than your device, your undivided attention tells people they're important to you.

Enhanced productivity. Do you really need constant access to your social notifications, Facebook updates, your email inbox, a bunch of tabs open in your web browser and all sorts of other things to feel in touch and in control? Accumulating interruptions steals peace of mind and minimizes your ability to get things done. Any time you're interrupted from a work-related task by something from your phone or computer, it can take as long as 45 minutes for your brain to refocus.

Mindfulness. When something interesting starts happening, what's your first reaction? Do you whip out your phone, start snapping photos and begin sharing on social media? Or do you savor the moment and delight in being in the moment? When you unplug, you force yourself to be more present.

"A natural side effect of unplugging is that you stop missing out on what you should be enjoying for yourself, rather than trying to tell everyone on social media about it," says author Elise Moreau.

ARE screens the problem or a symptom?

"It's become part of our culture to think that being too plugged in' and too dependent on our devices is the root of our problems, rather than a manifestation of other problems," says John Swartzberg, M.D.

"Is constantly checking your phone during dinner with your family causing you to be less close to them? Or are you constantly checking your phone because it's a convenient way to avoid conversations? Are you anxious and having trouble sleeping because you're spending too much time online? Or are you spending lots of time online to try to tune out your anxiety?" Swartzberg asks.

None of this is to say that he thinks it's a *good* thing that so many of us are so constantly connected to our devices.

"If we spend too much time staring at a screen, the life that is happening right in front of us—our kids' childhoods, conversations with our partners, work that we can do to help make the world better —may just pass us by."

CALL TO ACTION

Get to the heart of why you're spending so much time connected to technology. Isolate the benefits and issues, and then make a call whether you need to schedule the time to unplug.

Dive Deeper...

Take a real break from work—check out my interview in the New Zealand Herald, "Escape the Always On Culture," navigate to here —http://bit.ly/2s7PEWd

Learn polymath Tim Ferris's 4 steps to lifestyle design: definition, elimination, automation, and liberation. Watch it here: http://bit.ly/1nTs7jq

32

MASSAGE

"Massage has had a positive effect on every medical condition we've looked at."

~ Tiffany Field, Ph. D.

ONE OF MY favorite ways to rest is to go for a massage; but, so many people mistakenly think massage is an indulgence rather than a health-behavior.

Some of the many benefits of massage include reduced stress and higher levels of neuroendocrine and immune functioning—which means better hormonal balance and more immunity to disease and illness.

Some studies also suggest that a one-hour massage results in benefits equivalent to a 6-hour sleep.

Sounds good to me, especially when I'm feeling fatigued.

If getting naked isn't your thing, consider an energy healing treatment with a trained Reiki practitioner.

Reiki is a Japanese word. **Rei** means *universal transcendental spirit* and **Ki** stands for *life energy*. Hence, the word carries the sense of universal life energy. Many scientific minds, as well as sage healers, have throughout the years believed that the universe is filled with this invisible life energy, and life and health of all living beings is sustained by it.

HEALING hands

Increasing evidence suggests that there does exist a superior *intelligent force* which contains all creation and out of which all life arises. The energy of this force pervades everything and this is the energy that flows through our hands in concentrated form when we treat with Reiki.

Reiki healing is the ancient art of "hands-on healing" and offers a natural and holistic approach to mental, emotional, physical, and spiritual well-being.

You don't have to believe in any religion or be particularly spiritual to benefit from Reiki. It's an inclusive, non-religious form of healing and safe for everyone.

When I was experiencing a huge period of stress, I gained so much immediate benefit from my Reiki treatments that I decided to learn this beautiful healing technique. Recently in Bali, I completed my master level training.

You don't have to be Reiki-trained to live by the principles developed by Reiki founder Dr. Mikao Usui: "Just for today do not worry. Just for today do not anger. Honor your parents, teachers, and elders. Earn your living honestly. Show gratitude to everything."

CALL TO ACTION

Give yourself the gift of a therapeutic massage or Reiki treatment.

33

YOGA

"Between stimulus and response there is a space. In that space is our power to choose our response. In our response lies our growth and our freedom."

~ Viktor E. Frankl

"MY SON TOLD me I was a bad father," Wayan, a former bank employee, told me while I was on a recent trip to Bali. "It shocked me because I knew it was true. I was so stressed at work I went home and yelled and threw things around the house. After my son said that to me I went to work and resigned the next day."

Now a yoga teacher, Wayan is a dedicated believer in the power of yoga to de-stress your life and help you to relax and live a happier, healthier life.

Yoga, relaxation, and mindfulness practices work behind-the-scenes to help lower the stress hormone cortisol.

Just two 90-minute classes a week is enough to notice an improved stress response, even in those who report being highly distressed, according to research on yoga and meditation coming out of Germany. Study participants noted a decrease in stress, anxiety, and depression.

I came across the following quote, source unknown, and it seems to summarize the key benefits of yoga—flexibility...in body, mind, and spirit: "Blessed are the flexible, for they shall not be bent out of shape."

Yoga classes don't have to be difficult. They can vary from gentle and soothing to strenuous and challenging; the choice of style tends to be based on personal preference and physical ability.

Hatha yoga is the most common type of yoga practiced in the United States and combines three elements: physical poses, called *asanas*; controlled breathing practiced in conjunction with asanas; and a short period of deep relaxation or meditation.

"Available reviews of a wide range of yoga practices suggest they can reduce the impact of exaggerated stress responses and may be helpful for both anxiety and depression. In this respect, yoga functions like other self-soothing techniques, such as meditation, relaxation, exercise, or even socializing with friends," says an article posted by Harvard Medical School.

"By reducing perceived stress and anxiety, yoga appears to modulate stress response systems. This, in turn, decreases physiological arousal — for example, reducing the heart rate, lowering blood pressure, and easing respiration. There is also evidence that yoga practices help increase heart rate variability, an indicator of the body's ability to respond to stress more flexibly."

Researchers at the Walter Reed Army Medical Center in Washington, D.C., are offering a yogic method of deep relaxation to veterans returning from combat in Iraq and Afghanistan. Dr. Kristie Gore, a psychologist at Walter Reed, says the military hopes that yoga-based treatments will be more acceptable to the soldiers and less stigmatizing than traditional psychotherapy. The center now uses yoga and yogic relaxation in post-deployment PTSD awareness courses and plans to conduct a controlled trial of their effectiveness in the future.

Here are a few of the many reported benefits of yoga:

• Improvements in perceived stress, depression, anxiety, energy, fatigue, and well-being
• Reduced tension, anger, and hostility
• Reduced headaches and back pain
• Improved sleep quality
• Improved breathing and deeper relaxation

"Samskara saksat karanat purvajati jnanam. Through sustained focus and meditation on our patterns, habits, and conditioning, we gain knowledge and understanding of our past and how we can change the patterns that aren't serving us to live more freely and fully." ~ Yoga Sutra III.18

Call to Action

Nurture your body and soul with regular yoga sessions.

To FIND out more about laughing yoga check out this link http://laughteryoga.org.nz/the-story-of-laughter-yoga/

34

ELEVATE YOUR ENERGY

"The key to success is to raise your own energy; when you do, people will naturally be attracted to you."

~ Stuart Wilde, author

EVERYTHING IS ENERGY, and energy is everything. Without it you have nothing. But you don't want sad, bad, defeatist energy—that won't help at all.

Passion, joy, and love are the highest vibrations you can feel. They're the rocket-fuel feelings that will catapult you to success.

"The two most inspiring life forces are anger and joy," singer-songwriter Alanis Morissette once said. "I could write 6 zillion songs about these two feelings alone."

As you'll discover in my earlier book, *Find Your Passion and Purpose: Four Easy Steps to Discover a Job You Want and Live the Life You Love*, and later in this book, anger can be a constructive force for positive change.

But the more moments you spend being happy and joyful, and

allowing yourself and your work to be infused with this positive energy, the closer you are to being the God force of all life. You evoke the power of the laws of attraction and abundance, and you attract prosperity.

"If you will live your life in such a manner—that everything you pursue is to make yourself happy—you will live your life to its grandest destiny," writes Ramtha in *The White Book.*

"Joy begets joy, for when you accept the joy that is pressed to you, that joy heightens the joy of your tomorrows and opens you up for ever greater receivership."

Co-creating with joy, passion, Spirit, and love and creating and maintaining a positive mindset are essential ingredients in raising your productive energy.

Don't worry if you don't know what makes you happy or feel joyful or you haven't figured out where your passions lie. You'll dive deeper into this treasure trove of riches as you progress through this book.

What matters now is that you begin with the end in mind and make a commitment to only invest in things that make you feel good and create positive vibrations.

This may require doing some inner work, increasing your self-awareness and committing to further personal development. It may mean regularly checking in and monitoring your calibration. Or it may involve some tough action.

Many successful people choose to walk away from soul-sucking jobs and relationships to elevate their energy. Paulo Coelho, Isabel Allende, J.K Rowling, Nora Roberts, James Patterson, and Jessie Burton, for example, may not have read Ramtha's sage words which I have quoted below, but they found success by pursuing the love, joy, and passion they discovered when writing.

Importantly, in the process of following their bliss, they all rekindled a deep love for themselves.

"There is no greater purpose in life than to live for the love and fulfilment of self, and that can only be achieved by participating in this life and doing those things which bring you happiness regardless of what they are, for who shall say it is wrong or that it is not good for you?" writes Ramtha in *The White Book*.

Call to Action

What daily practices, routines, or habits fill you with joy? Notice the times you feel marvelous.

What soul-sucking jobs, relationships, or situations depress your energy?

How can you manifest feel-good vibrations? Develop a plan to restore positivity to your daily diet.

35

DO LESS, ACHIEVE MORE

"Remember that just because you're doing a lot more doesn't mean you're getting a lot more done. Don't confuse movement with progress. My mother told me, she said: 'Yeah because you can run in one place all the time and never get anywhere.'"

~ Denzel Washington, actor

TAKING time out is a spiritual principle taught very well in the Bible, but even the most spiritual people often feel they are worthless unless they are doing something every waking hour of the day, connected with everyone on all the social media platforms, and incessantly checking their emails.

Yet if you look back at some of the symptoms of stress, you will see that peoples' cognitive or thinking capabilities actually reduce. Stressed people make more mistakes, forget more, and take longer to achieve less.

So, taking a holiday or scaling back your workload is a great way to revitalize your performance and to work smarter, not harder.

When I was feeling stressed many years ago following a period of intense personal and professional change, I knew I needed time out. At first, I didn't think I could afford it. Instead of staying stuck I started to think proactively. I asked my higher self, "How can I afford a break?"

I rented out my house to short-term holiday people on holiday-homes.com. While people were staying in my house, I stayed at a friend's holiday house—rent free.

I rescheduled all my appointments and cleared my diary for three weeks.

While away I scheduled no more than two hours a day for work-related activities. I couldn't afford to go completely cold turkey, but at least I avoided working my normal 12-hour days. I made sure I minimized interruptions by turning off my phone and shutting down the laptop.

As I write this chapter, I have just returned from a digital-detox holiday in Bali. Stepping away from technology for three-weeks has been a wonder-cure for my productivity.

CALL TO ACTION

How could you schedule some time out? Add this to your stress-busting plan discussed at the end of this book.

36

AROMATHERAPY FOR MENTAL ALERTNESS

"If you believe in aromatherapy...it works! If you don't believe in aromatherapy...it works!"

~ Cristina Proano-Carrion, aromatherapist

ALONG WITH YOUR skills and capabilities, it is your state of mind that determines how productive, successful and happy you will be.

There are many ways to empower your mind—working with essential oils is one of the most effortless. The sense of smell is the most basic and primitive of all our senses and is of vital importance to your well-being.

The process of smelling is called olfaction and is incredibly complicated, taking place in several areas of the brain including the limbic system which itself has approximately 34 structures and 53 pathways. The limbic system is linked to sensations of pleasure and pain, and emotions— both positive and negative, including fear and confidence, sadness and joy and other feelings that can either erode or boost productivity and prosperity.

The simple truth is, even if you are unaware of the power of smell, aroma affects your mood.

Scientists now believe that all of our emotions are the result of neurochemicals such as noradrenaline and serotonin being released into the bloodstream, and mood swings are thought to be a result of these influences, particularly when they are in the extreme.

Given these facts, it's not hard to see how essential oils can help balance and influence our thoughts, feelings, and behaviors.

"Feeling educated about essential oils is such an empowering experience because there are so many different oils you can work with," writes Clinical Aromatherapist Andrea Butje in her book, *The Heart of Aromatherapy: An Easy-to-Use Guide for Essential Oils.*

"They all offer the nourishment of the plant they are distilled from in a single drop, and education helps you understand which oils to reach for at which times. Nature works holistically...and so do we."

As I share in my book, *The Art of Success: How Extraordinary Artists Can Help You Succeed in Business and Life,* Coco Chanel knew the alchemical potency of flowers and plants. She surrounded herself with nature's elixir and amassed a fortune from the essential oils which helped make her perfume Chanel N°5 famous.

"A woman who doesn't wear perfume has no future," Coco Chanel once said.

The transcendent alchemy of the potions that went into the Chanel N°5 formula was not left to chance. Grieving after her lover Boy Chapel's death, Coco drew upon the essences of jasmine, ylang ylang, vetiver, and other restorative scents to imbue Coco's Chanel N°5 with hope, healing, and the sensual confidence that love lost would be found again.

Aromatherapy, using the scents of plants and flowers, is one of many ancient remedies validated by modern science today. It's the Swiss army knife of all things healing—physically, mentally, spiritually, and emotionally.

There are so many different essential oils that can help you. Here are a few essential oils and natural therapeutic remedies to help increase your alertness and refresh and uplift your mind, body, and spirit:

1.) Laurel Essential Oil: Motivates people who lack energy or confidence. It also strengthens the memory and helps maintain concentration, especially during prolonged tasks

2.) Rosemary Essential Oil: Instills confidence during periods of self-doubt and keeps motivation levels high when the going gets tough. It is also said to help maintain an open mind and to make you more welcoming of new ideas.

3.) Cardamom Essential Oil: Stimulates a dull mind, dispels tensions and worries, and nurtures and supports the brain and nervous system. Many people find it of great support during challenging times.

4.) Peppermint Essential Oil: With its refreshing scent peppermint works like a power boost for your fatigued mind, making you feel sharper and more alert.

ALERTNESS:

- Ginger 6 drops
- Grapefruit 5 drops
- Juniper Berry 4 drops
- 15 ml of a carrier oil

Energizing:

- Lavender 8 drops
- Lemon 2 drops
- Orange 6 drops
- Rosemary 4 drops

Aromatherapy for emotional well-being

The use of essential oils for emotional well-being is what is often first thought of when someone thinks of the term "aromatherapy."

Although aromatherapy should not be considered a miracle cure for serious emotional issues, the use of essential oils can assist, sometimes greatly, with particular emotional issues.

For example, lavender is a well-known mild analgesic, useful for healing headaches, wounds, calming the nerves, insomnia, and mild depression.

Rosemary, on the other hand, is a mild stimulant and is used to treat physical and mental fatigue, forgetfulness, and respiratory problems among other ailments.

STRESS-RELIEVING BLENDS

THESE BLENDS STATED below can help during times of stress. When selecting and using oils, be sure to follow all safety precautions and remember that aromatherapy should not be used as a substitute for proper medical treatment.

Blend #1

- Three drops Clary Sage, one drop Lemon, one drop Lavender

Blend #2

- Two drops Romance Chamomile, two drops Lavender, one drop Vetiver

Blend #3

- Three drops Bergamot, one drop Geranium, one drop Frankincense

Blend #4

- Three drops Grapefruit, one drop Jasmine, one drop Ylang Ylang

DIRECTIONS:

1. Select one of the blends shown above.
2. Choose which method you'd like to use the blend and follow the directions below:

DIFFUSER BLEND

Multiply your blend by four to obtain a total of 20 drops of your chosen blend. Add your oils to a dark colored glass bottle and mix well by rolling the bottle in between your hands. Add the appropriate number of drops from your created blend to your diffuser by following the manufacturer's instructions.

BATH OIL:

Multiply your blend by three to obtain a total of 15 drops of your chosen blend.

Bath Salts:

Continue by using the five drops, blend with Bath Salts.

Massage Oil:

Multiply your blend by two to obtain a total of 10 drops of your chosen blend.

Air Freshener:

Multiply your blend by six to obtain a total of 30 drops of your chosen blend.

Call to Action

Investigate the power of smell. Read more about aromatherapy for achievers and learn about essential oils for success.

What scents imbue you with confidence? Courage? Productivity? Sharpen your most potent tools—your heart and your mind. Become a perfumer—experiment with essential oils until you find a winning blend.

Create your own success blend, or have an expert create one for you. Beginning with how you want to feel is a good place to start.

37

COLOR THERAPY FOR EMOTIONAL WELL-BEING

"I cannot pretend to feel impartial about colors. I rejoice with the brilliant ones and am genuinely sorry for the poor browns."

~ Winston Churchill

COLOR HAS a profound effect on us at all levels - physical, mental, emotional, and spiritual.

We are in a world where color dominates our lives, from reading signs on the road to identifying ripe fruit by its color.

Color affects our moods - blue is calming - red can make us tense. We use color every day in our lives without even appreciating it.

Decide on the mood you want to be in and choose a color that makes you feel that way. For example, if you want to feel calm, you may choose green or blue.

Remember that color is individually perceived, so choose what works for you. On some days red may make you feel energized, on others it may fuel feelings of anger or aggression.

You may want to wear your stress-busting color in your clothes, or just to have a small dose of color nearby to prompt these feelings along – for example, it may be some color on your desktop or on a prompt card by your PC or in your wallet.

Wearing color also sparks joy in others. As a shop assistant recently said to me, "You have just made my day with how pink and sparkly you are."

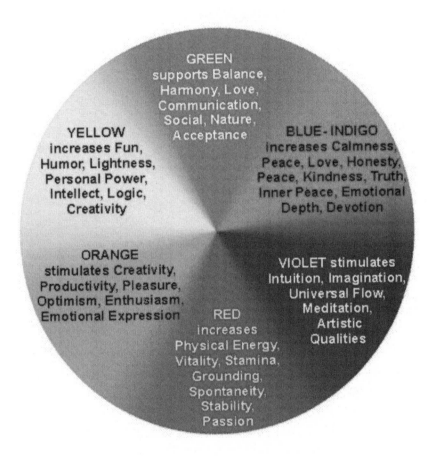

CALL TO ACTION

Surround yourself with colors that spark joy and banish those that don't.

38

LAUGH

"I love people who can smile in trouble."

~ Leonardo da Vinci

INJECT some more laughter into your life. Laughter and humor are great tonics during stressful times.

"Discovering more joy does not, I'm sorry to say, save us from the inevitability of hardship and heartbreak. In fact, we may cry more easily, but we will laugh more easily, too," says Archbishop Desmond Tutu in *The Book of Joy*.

"Perhaps we are just more alive. Yet as we discover more joy, we can face suffering in a way that ennobles rather than embitters. We have hardship without becoming hard. We have heartbreak without being broken."

Taking yourself or your life too seriously only increases stress. When you learn to laugh in spite of your difficulties, you light up the world.

"When people just look at your face," the Dalai Lama said to the

Archbishop, "You are always laughing, always joyful. This is a very positive message."

CALL TO ACTION

You may not feel like it, but give laughter a go. Watch a funny movie, stream a stack of whacky comedies, go to a comedy show, or watch a clip on YouTube. Hang out with people who know how to have a good time, go to a Laughing Yoga class, or ask someone to tickle you!

39

PLAY

"Creativity is intelligence having fun."

~ Albert Einstein

"Too much of our work amounts to the drudgery of arranging means toward ends, mechanically placing the right foot in front of the left and the left in front of the right, moving down narrow corridors toward narrow goals," writes author James Ogilvy.

"Play widens the halls. Work will always be with us, and many works are worthy. But the worthiest works of all often reflect an artful creativity that looks more like play than work," Ogilvy says.

Be playful. Cultivate your inner child. Don't take yourself too seriously. Act up a little, goof-off, experiment, relax and detach—if you find yourself in trouble, smile.

Laughter triggers the release of endorphins, the brain's feel good chemicals, setting off an emotional reaction which makes us feel great.

"It is much better when there is not too much seriousness," said

His Holiness the Dalai Lama. "Laughter, joking is much better. Then we can be completely relaxed. I met some scientists in Japan, and they explained that wholehearted laughter—not artificial laughter— is very good for your heart and your health in general."

BENEFITS OF PLAY INCLUDE:

- Increasing your productivity
- Boosting your creativity and problem-solving skills
- Reducing stress, anxiety, and depression
- Improving your relationships and connections with others
- Bringing more balance, fun, lightness and levity into your life
- Diminishing your worries

As play researcher and psychiatrist Stuart Brown says in his book *Play: How it Shapes the Brain, Opens the Imagination, and Invigorates the Soul*, "A lack of play should be treated like malnutrition: it's a health risk to your body and mind."

Some of the many ways I play include: "wagging" work sometimes and taking my inner child on a playdate to the movies, going for a massage, or indulging in my hobbies and playing with my paints. Listening to music from the 70s is also playful and brings levity. While travelling internationally recently, I watched the Disney children's movie *Frozen*. I haven't laughed so much in years.

I also love reminding myself of the magic of writing. As novelist Caroline Gordon once wrote, "A well-composed book is a magic carpet on which we are wafted to a world that we cannot enter in any other way."

Author Deepak Chopra confirms the power of lightening up: You may not feel like it, but give laughter a go. Watch a funny movie, stream a stack of whacky comedies, go to a comedy show, or watch a clip on YouTube. Hang out with people who know how to have a good time, go to a Laughing Yoga class, or ask someone to tickle you!

"When we harness the forces of harmony, joy and love, we create success and good fortune with effortless ease."

CALL TO ACTION

How can you be more playful—at home and at work?

What benefits will flow?

CHECK out my blog for some strategies to reinforce play —http://bit.ly/29RPQis

40

FIND YOUR VIBE TRIBE

"When you choose to step out of limiting thoughts and listen to
the song in your heart, you'll find the people who want to share
and celebrate the journey with you. You'll find your tribe."

~ Dr. Julie Connor, author

THE SIMPLEST DEFINITION of a tribe is a group of people that share the
same language, customs, beliefs—and aspirations.

As you've already discovered, sometimes to flourish you need to
break free of your current tribe and find one that fuels your dreams
and brings out the best in you.

Your vibe tribe is a great team of others—whether they be significant friends, partners, or family members, or those found online
through wonderful Facebook groups and webinars.

I found my vibe tribe online. We have never met in person, but we
stay connected and share success strategies via Facebook, and occasionally we link-up on video conferencing calls.

As I write this chapter, a member of my vibe tribe, Scott Allen, who is the author of many brilliant books about living fearlessly, sent me a PDF of his successful book launch strategy. This is a powerful example of being co-creators in one another's mutual success.

My vibe tribe also finds me—reaching out to me after enjoying my books. Many of my readers love to help me co-create prosperity by reading advance copies of my new books and contributing valuable feedback.

This feedback, and the positive reviews on Amazon and via the online communities I have created for my readers on Facebook, sustains me and encourages me to keep writing. I love hearing their success stories.

Other readers have helped me grow my vibe tribe by interviewing me on their podcasts and success summits. Recently, Sheree Clark, a fabulous and influential healthy-living coach based in the US, discovered my book *Mid-life Career Rescue: The Call for Change* and showcased it on American television. She also included an interview with me in her fabulous "What the Fork" summit. You'll find a link to this interview and the TV clip on my media page at www.cassandragaisford.com/media.

Successful authors and podcasters like Tim Ferris (tim.blog/podcast) and Joanna Penn (www.thecreativepenn.com) found their vibe tribes by following their enthusiasms. They created their vibes by following their passionate purposes to share what they learn with others.

Here's a few ways to find a vibe tribe:

- Scan Facebook for like-minded groups
- Enroll in a writing course—they often include a private members group on social media
- Create a Facebook community of your own—show up and encourage others
- Listen to podcasts which inspire you to become the best version of you—Joanna Penn's podcast is very helpful for

"authorpreneurs." I also love Neil Patel's podcast for savvy marketing strategies: http://neilpatel.com/podcast. Tim Ferriss' podcast is also always inspiring http://tim.blog/podcast.

- Join writers' groups and become an active member of writing bodies—romance writers, for example, gain huge encouragement from The Romance Writers of America, Australia and New Zealand. These professional groups are dedicated to helping their members thrive. They offer courses to learn new skills from established authors; the chance to enter competitions where you can gain valuable feedback (or win!); conferences at which to network, meet agents and pitch your books—and much more encouragement
- Check out Meetup.com and find a group of like-mined souls to meet up with in person
- Speak from your heart, write with passion and purpose, and send your love letters to the world via your books, blogs, podcasts, or other mediums, including social media

If you are having trouble solving problems, there are many networks within the community that can assist you. This could be your local Church, the Life Line Service, or the services your Local Council offers to the community, e.g., Citizens Advice Bureau.

Your own friends and family could also be a great help if you are willing listen to their suggestions.

Remember, "A problem shared is a problem halved." Gather a team of supportive or like-minded people who will nourish your burning desire, cheerlead, and support you when you feel flat or overwhelmed and elevate your success.

CALL TO ACTION

How can you develop an encouraging network of friends and acquaintances?

How can you remove yourself from people who don't encourage or support your dreams?

Who can you reach out to during times of need?

41

MONITOR YOUR TIME

"Go after whatever gives you meaning in life and trust yourself to handle whatever it takes."

~ Kelly McGonigal, health psychologist

ACTIVITY LOGS ARE a great way to keep track of your time and to see clearly where you are wasting it.

Using the following log, make a list of everything you do, and the time you take to do it.

Analyze it after two-three weeks. Identify and eliminate time-wasting and low-yield jobs. Identify more efficient ways to working.

If you have multiple income streams and demands on your time, you may prefer to set up an excel sheet and color code your activities.

I've done this recently and love it. Color coding allows me to quickly see time sucks, while monitoring holds me more personally accountable.

DATE

TIME

ACTIVITY

Wᴀʏs ᴛᴏ ᴘʀɪᴏʀɪᴛɪᴢᴇ ᴛɪᴍᴇ:

- **Keep a "to do" list:** Break up large tasks into smaller task. Allocate priorities from A (very important) to F (unimportant). When you have several tasks of similar priority, number them in order of priority; i.e., B2 may be the second most important B priority task.
- **Delegate:** Work out the value of skills and time – delegate lower value tasks to others; contract in extra resources if needed
- **Negotiate** – try and find a mutually agreeable solution to time demands and work required by others
- **Take breaks** to refresh your mind. Rather than wasting time you will gain time by being more productive.
- **Develop systems** to help you organize yourself better. This will help you avoid wasting time looking for things or reinventing the wheel.
- **Set key objectives:** decide what your most important goals are and what you won't compromise on achieving. Then make a plan of everything you are going to have to do to achieve these objectives. Try not to do any tasks that won't lead you directly to achieving your key objectives. Become a creative procrastinator by putting off until tomorrow that which won't advance your goals today!
- **Allocate and schedule your time:** decide what constitutes a suitable balance of work-life time for you and allocate it

each week. How many hours for work? For family? For play? Set rules for yourself on how your time is used and try not to compromise. Jan, a single mother, negotiated with her daughter for time to herself. She scheduled "me time" into the scheduler of her mobile phone. At 9pm the alarm sounded telling everybody that she was now officially "unavailable."

- **Rest for peak performance:** Working harder not smarter is a key reason many people are stressed. Do less and achieve more.

CALL TO ACTION

Monitor you time and take back control.

42

CHANGE YOUR BRAIN WITH MUSIC

"I'm in an almost perpetual state of writer's block—writing is an occasional thing. What do I do about it? I drive around in my car and listen to music."

~ Aaron Sorkin, screenwriter

BOOST YOUR WINNING mindset by playing more music because it will stimulate you to new heights, help improve your brain functioning, and enable you to find creative answers and solutions to recurring challenges.

This may involve playing an instrument, perhaps by picking up one that you have studied in the past. It could also mean taking lessons.

Or it could just be a message for you to spend more time listening to music. Many people find it helpful to play music around their home and workplace continually.

"Music puts a spell on you," says author and intuitive coach Awen

Finn. "Deep inside your favorite song lay the secret messages that unlock your psyche and all your potential."

Be sure to listen to uplifting tunes, as you are sensitive to the words and melodies. You may want to sing in order to express the music that's within you.

Along with the "Prosperity Playlist" I've compiled on Spotify, one of my favorite music tools is an app found at <u>focusatwill.com</u>. I'm a big fan of this science-based tool. Not only do I love the music, but I love what it's doing for my productivity.

> "The question many people want answered is how they can maximize focus so that their environment becomes less distracting and their attentional spotlight is continuously focused on their projects of the day," writes the team of researchers, scientists, and psychologists at Focus@Will.
>
> "Auditory neuroscience and psychoacoustics (the psychology of sound perception) can help us answer this question," they say. "When you listen to music, sound waves hit your eardrums, are transferred to the cochlea in your inner ears, where microscopic cells called hair cells vibrate in response to the sound. The movement of the hair cells turns the mechanical energy of the sound wave into chemical signals that stimulate auditory nerves to fire action potentials."

Is this all too technical for you? Stay with us and learn how music can change the neurochemicals in your brain—and therefore, positively impact your mood and behavior.

> "Where does the signal go from there? The auditory pathway takes the encoded action potential signal from the ears to the brainstem cochlear nucleus and gets processed in a bunch of other brainstem locations. Finally, the signal moves to the thalamus and to the primary auditory cortex in the temporal lobe, which sits above your ears on each side of your head.
>
> "When the signal gets into the brainstem, before it goes to the

cortex and you become conscious of the sound, one of the areas that is likely to be activated is a bunch of neurons called the locus coeruleus. The locus coeruleus produces noradrenaline (also called norepinephrine), which is a stimulant for your brain.

"It sends noradrenaline to many other locations in your brain. The areas targeted by the locus coeruleus are responsible for deciding how you are going to respond to a stimulus."

BOTH HUMANS and animals respond to music. To relax effectively, listen to sounds of the sea, rainforest, running water, or classical music. Personally, I love listening to the wave music at calm.com.

Listening to soothing sounds will instantly calm the mind and body. Harmonious tunes prompt the brain to release a hormone, known as ACTH (adrenocorticotropic hormone), which has a calming effect on the body.

Call to Action

Create a soundtrack to feed your dreams. I still love Miley Cyrus's *The Climb*, particularly the encouraging lyrics to persist and persevere. "Ain't about how fast I get there. Ain't about what's waiting on the other side. It's the climb."

Consider working to a neuroscience-based soundtrack, or download an app like Focus@Will.

43

GET OUTSIDE

"This sun gives spirit and life to plants, and the earth nourishes them with moisture."

~ Leonardo da Vinci

WE ARE ALMOST LIKE PLANTS—WE need at least 20 minutes of sunlight every day just to make our hormones work effectively. Medical research suggests some people need as much as two hours a day of sunlight to avoid seasonal affective disorder.

Therefore, to feel and behave normally you need to be exposed to full-spectrum daylight on a regular basis. Experts recommend that you spend at least 20 minutes a day outside. Not only will you get the light you need, but you'll also recharge your batteries - making you more efficient when you return.

Walking outside can also help you gain a new perspective on a troubling situation. When you go outside and take a walk, you increase the electrical activity in your brain, and you breathe negative ions and see in three dimensions. All this helps with seeing things which are troubling you with fresh eyes.

Time alone engaging the whole brain will provide you with an opportunity to process things that are troubling you and to see things more objectively. Sometimes the situation is not as bad as it first appeared, or the solution is relatively simple.

Being amongst nature also sparks joy. When you feel joyful, you are accessing the right posterior parietal lobe portion of your brain. In order to activate this part of the brain, you have to be able to see in three dimensions.

Many people spend hours in front of two-dimensional computer monitors and TV screens, and then top off a 12-hour day at work by trying to read themselves to sleep on their Kindle - all two-dimensional visual activities.

CALL TO ACTION

Monitor how much time you spend indoors.

Schedule regular fresh air time.

Improve your breathing, and take a brisk walk to increase levels of oxygen.

44

REAL RESILIENCE

"A grit mind strengthens all of your strengths."

~ Pearl Zhu, digital visionary

UPS AND DOWNS, highs and lows, troughs and peaks are a rite of passage for everyone.

The fickleness and unpredictability of the world, the extremities of your emotions, the quick and ready insights you experience, the acute sensitivity with which you feel almost everything, can make you vulnerable.

But it doesn't have to be this way. By strengthening your inner power, your ability to handle stressful situations, and your skill in persevering after setbacks threaten to fell you, you'll develop resilient grit.

Grit comes in many shapes and sizes: courage, bravery, pluck, mettle, backbone, spirit, steel nerve, resolve, determination, endurance, guts, spunk, tenacity—and the strength of vulnerability.

Add the flexibility and determination of resilience and you'll have a winning combination.

Resilience is that indefinable quality that allows some people to be bowled over by life and re-emerge stronger than ever. Rather than letting setbacks overcome them and drain their resolve, they find a way to rise from the ashes.

Psychologists have identified some of the factors that will make you more resilient, among them a positive attitude, optimism, the ability to regulate emotions, and the ability to see failure as a form of helpful feedback.

Life will keep throwing you curveballs— it may even, at times, drown you in a deluge of seemingly never-ending hassles—family dramas, environmental mayhem, world affairs, or some other toxin.

As Buddhists say, life is suffering—it's how you react to a setback that counts. We choose our attitude via our thoughts. "With our thoughts, we make the world," Buddha once said.

Many of the strategies I've shared with you in this book will help you develop a resilient mindset and with it more staying power, passion, perseverance, and grit.

Mindfulness techniques, avoiding excessive alcohol consumption, keeping your thoughts positive, surrounding yourself with a vibe tribe of positive supporters, getting rid of toxicity (friends, family, or stinkin' thinkin'), meditating, exercise, reprogramming your subconscious beliefs, and other strategies are just some of the things you've learned in *Stress Less. Love Life More: How to Stop Worrying, Reduce Anxiety, Eliminate Negative Thinking and Find Happiness.*

But, as someone said to me recently, "Life's hard enough without having to do all this 'feel good' stuff." That, dear reader, comes down to choice. Your choice.

Personally, I don't want to live, nor end my life, as F. Scott Fitzgerald did—a poor drunk who felt like a failure and only found success when he was dead.

I don't want to lie in my grave like Amy Winehouse, a dead, tortured "success" at 27. According to hypnotherapist Marisa Peer, who said Winehouse had cancelled an appointment with her, she had refused to change her mindset. What a sad and tragic waste of talent and potential.

It's not easy to overcome many of the things that hold you back. But you can do it—if you're willing to be strong and fight for your dreams. Within many of us lies an innate seam of strength, which, when mined skilfully, will produce an endless source of pure gold.

As author and filmmaker Michael Moore said, "I want us all to face our fears and stop behaving like our goal in life is merely to survive. Surviving is for game show contestants stranded in the jungle or on a desert island. You are not stranded. Use your power. You deserve better."

I took these words to heart many years ago. Anxiety and depression run in my family—as does a tendency to place a stop-cap on dreams. My grandmother grew up in foster care. Her father murdered a man. I'm sure that her upbringing had an impact on my mom, and in turn, my mom's ability to give me the love I craved as a child.

My dad was dumped in a boarding school when he was only four. He never knew his father, and only found out when he was in his 70s that he had a sister. Growing up, he never experienced a hug or knew true affection.

Like Amy Winehouse and so many others with wounded childhoods, I never felt loved. I've worked hard to overcome the wounds of my childhood.

You should, too. Your past doesn't need to stop you.

"A lot of people feel like they're victims in life, and they'll often point to past events, perhaps growing up with an abusive parent or in a dysfunctional family," writes Rhonda Byrne in *The Secret*.

"Most psychologists believe that about 85 percent of families are dysfunctional, so all of a sudden you're not so unique. My parents were alcoholics. My dad abused me. My mother divorced him when I was six . . . I mean, that's almost everybody's story in some form or not," she says.

Author Jack Canfield also speaks to this point: "The real question is, what are you going to do now? What do you choose now? Because you can either keep focusing on that, or you can focus on what you want. And when people start focusing on what they want, what they don't want falls away, and what they want expands, and the other part disappears."

In hindsight, you will see your life experiences as a gift. As Isabel Allende once said, "Without my unhappy childhood and dysfunctional family, what would I have to write about?"

I channel my life experiences into my books. I pay it forward and share how I learned to empower my mind, body, and soul. I studied Buddhist philosophy. I learned Transcendental and mindfulness meditation.

I devoured nearly every self-help book on the planet—and beyond. I went to healers and sought counseling.

I trained to be a hypnotherapist, counselor, and psychologist, and gained other therapeutic skills. I continue to pass on the knowledge I've learned to my clients and readers like you to help empower them to live their best lives.

Every day I fight for my dreams.

We all enter this life, and leave it, with different challenges. Different parents, siblings, life experiences. The pain of your past doesn't need to define you. If you are prepared to be honest and vulnerable and to do the work, you know what you need to do to empower your life and your work.

As Buddha once said, "It is better to conquer yourself than to win a thousand battles. Then the victory is yours. It cannot be taken from you, not by angels or by demons, heaven or hell."

CALL TO ACTION

If fear, wounds of the past, victim thinking, destructive health behaviors, or anything else detrimental to living your best life has a grip on you, prioritize breaking free.

Seeking help doesn't have to cost a fortune. You may heal your life with writing, work with a coach or therapist, or self-help your way to success.

When you seize the reins of control and take responsibility, you will empower your life, your joy, and your prosperity.

45

KEEP LEARNING

"I love those who can smile in trouble, who can gather strength from distress, and grow brave by reflection. 'Tis the business of little minds to shrink, but they whose heart is firm, and whose conscience approves their conduct, will pursue their principles unto death."

~ Leonardo da Vinci

Contrary to what some people may believe, taking time out to boost your motivation and self-belief is an extremely cost-effective and productive use of time.

As one person wrote to me recently, "I just took an hour and watched your interview with Ande Anderson on the *Truth about Prosperity* summit; thank you, it was once again inspirational and motivating. I am whisking along on my new idea, getting stuck, getting unstuck, tripping over, getting up and all the while loving every moment. There is so much to learn."

Similarly, a person who had read the first book in the series wrote, "WOW. I can't wait to read the whole book. These books just keep on giving me the motivation and a constant feeling of being connected with others while working away on my own. Very cool."

Here are just a few ways to fuel your verve:

✓ Conferences
✓ Podcasts
✓ Ted Talks
✓ Seminars
✓ Books
✓ Webinars
✓ Workshops

CALL TO ACTION

How can you fuel your passion, belief motivation, and tenacity to succeed?

What do you need to learn more of, less of, stop or start learning?

Make investing in continual learning part of your success strategy.

DIVE DEEPER...

Empower your millionaire mindset and think your way to success with book one of the Prosperity for Authors series, *Developing A Millionaire Mindset*. Available in print and ebook from Amazon here —getBook.at/TheProsperousAuthor.

Discover how to accent the positive, change your brain with music, cultivate hope, chase the light, and develop patient perseverance.

46

SUMMARY OF HOLISTIC COPING
STRATEGIES

Throughout this book you've discovered ways to reduce the stress response by increasing your ability to cope (e.g., regular exercise, good diet, relaxation exercises, and rest).
Listed below are some helpful reminders of some of the many holistic copy strategies you can call upon during times of current or anticipated need.

PHYSICAL

- Learn to listen to your body
- Adequate exercise
- Sport
- Physical touch / sex
- Muscle relaxation
- Sleep
- Warmth
- Relaxation breathing

- Healthy diet i.e. reducing stimulants (coffee, nicotine etc), increasing water, and eating organic non-processed foods
- Massage
- Yoga

BEHAVIOURAL

- Balanced lifestyle
- Support groups / Counseling
- Sharing with friends and family
- Humor
- New interests / activities
- Hobbies
- Socializing
- Entertaining
- Taking time out
- Music / dancing / singing
- Meditating
- Yoga
- Being proactive and taking control of the situation
- Change careers
- Reduce or eliminate alcohol consumption
- Reduce or eliminate caffeinated drinks
- Relax—make time to do nothing at all

COGNITIVE / **Perceptual (thinking)**

- Rational thinking techniques to help change the way you

interpret the stressful situation, thereby reducing the perception of threat (i.e. CBT)

- Positive thinking
- Self-assertion training
- Personal development
- Building self-esteem
- Realistic goal planning
- Time management
- Learning to say "No"
- Priority clarification
- Reflection
- Mindfulness
- Acceptance

EMOTIONAL

- Releasing emotions and expressing feelings (laugh, talk, cry, write in a journal, paint etc.)
- Learning how to "switch off"
- Taking time out
- Solitude and space
- Intimacy
- Counseling and support
- Challenging your emotional reactions to situations

Social

- Scheduling time to spend with important people in your life

- Making plans with friends, family and loved ones in advance
- Sharing your experiences of stress with certain people in your life, especially letting them know the ways that stress has been affecting you so that they know where you are coming from
- Practicing assertive communication within your significant relationships to decrease conflicts, while also continuing to find ways to show people around you that they are important

Spiritual

- Prayer—scheduling regular time
- Meditation—scheduling regular time
- Helping others (talking, writing, supporting etc.)
- Reiki and energy healing techniques
- Talking with a spiritual confidant or leader to explain any spiritual issues or doubts that you may have encountered
- Forgiveness (of self or other)
- Compassion / loving kindness
- Continuing to read and learn about your faith, belief or value system
- Connecting with others who share your beliefs

CAN you think of any others?

47

YOUR STRESS MANAGEMENT AND BUILDING RESILIENCE PLAN

Reflect back on the strategies and tools you've discovered in this book. Complete the following exercise to create your personal action plan for managing stress and building resilience:

Personal Action Plan for Managing Stress and Building Resilience

- Factors in your work and life that are causing you the greatest stress are:

- The four coping strategies which you know work for you in dealing with stress are:

- Your no-excuses strategy to make a commitment to put

one or more of these strategies into practice at least once a
day is:.

- The positive phrase you will use to help change your level
of stress is:

- Put this phrase where you can see it and say it to yourself
when you start to feel stressed.

COMPLETE THE FOLLOWING:

I SHALL STOP DOING:

I SHALL DO LESS:

I SHALL DO MORE:

I SHALL START TO DO:

REMEMBER ANGRY MARTIN? Eventually he sought career counseling
and developed a stress management plan to help him build a strong
foundation for success. A few of the changes he made included:

HE STARTED: running; eating organic foods; meditating; reading self-empowerment books; working on a plan for career fulfillment; pushing back on unreasonable client demands; taking quiet time out for himself and spending time alone in nature.

HE STOPPED: working weekends; drinking alcohol; watching TV; reading negative media; responding to emails and texts and calls immediately; working with clients he didn't enjoy; complaining; angry, explosive rants and raves; infecting everyone else with his bad moods; blaming others.

HE DID LESS: work after hours; Facebook surfing; drinking coffee; emails—picking up the phone instead; saying no to social get-togethers; spending money he hadn't yet earned.

HE DID MORE: focusing on what was going well and listing gratitudes; taking control of the things he could influence; spending time in the garden; planning holidays and quality time with his son; taking time out to focus on his hobbies and passions; controlling his emotions; taking responsibility; creating systems and templates that allowed him to work smarter not harder; and delegating.

I HOPE this chapter has given you some tools to deal effectively with any stress you may be suffering and also reminds you of the need to make positive changes in your life.

YOU MAY NEED to refer to this chapter again as you prepare to make changes in the future.

AFTERWORD

I hope you have found a few useful tips in this book to help you conquer stress and fuel greater resilience. Mastering the ability to slay stress dragons lies at the heart of your mental, emotional, spiritual, and physical well-being.

Managing stress effectively will single-handedly boost your happiness and success, and fan the embers of your desires to help you live your best life. The world needs you and eagerly awaits the fulfillment of your dreams!

I always believe that I should practice what I preach and so you can be sure that many of the strategies and techniques I have shared with you are ones I have put into practice myself. Writing this book is a case in point. It really was a case of putting all that I knew into practice—once again.

This book is a labor of love, passion, and purpose. One that had its seeds in the culmination and intersection of my talents, my interests, my motivations, and external drivers. Life kept telling me that this was a book I not only wanted to write, but was called to write.

An email from a reader who discovered one of my earlier blogs on stress provided a compelling reminder to crack on and take this book from my archives.

External factors also spurred my motivation, like juggling work, running multiple businesses, renovating a neglected house on a 10-acre property, supporting my partner through family dramas—and then, as if I wasn't "stressed" enough, a violent, trespasser intruded upon what little peace of mind I had managed to salvage.

So, yes—life is stressful. Sometimes exceedingly stressful. I've discovered first-hand just how essential it is to build resilience ahead of time. I hope you have, too.

I've also learned to revalue the spiritually-motivating power of living to a purpose and strengthened my intuitive powers in the process.

I've been inspired by the American singer, Meatloaf. His mission to find a producer for his album *Bat Out of Hell* is such an inspirational story about passion, grit, perseverance, failure, and ultimate success.

Plus, I've followed one of my muses, Richard Branson, whose wise words, "If it's not fun I'm not doing it," have reminded me to always work with joy.

Follow Your Joy

What is my joy? Well, I have several, but one of the most important is that by writing this book I have helped you gain the clarity, confidence, courage and inspiration to live a happy, healthy life and to follow your dreams.

I dream that you, and those you love, can be truly happy at work, and that your happiness will spread the seeds of joy amongst all you meet.

I dream that one day the current research that states that less than 10% of people are living their passions will be surpassed by new data showing that over 80% of people are happy at work and in life.

Is this really dreaming? Decide for yourself. Perhaps, this book will help you to turn your dreams of a happy working life into a fulfilling reality.

Thank you for allowing me to go on this journey with you. Wishing you everything your heart desires.

Passionately and happily yours,
Cassandra

P.S. What makes you happy?
I feel passionately about the need for more happiness at work. Mentally, physically, emotionally, and spiritually, work consumes a large part of your life. If you want to succeed and you want to be healthy—you need to do what makes you happy. You know this, right? But you may be like some of my readers who have lost sight of their strengths and what gives them joy.

In response to this feedback, I wrote a second book in the *Mid-Life Career Rescue* series called, *What Makes You Happy.* It became an instant #1 best-seller on Amazon.

In *What Makes You Happy,* I'll help you clarify what you need from work to be fulfilled. Plus we'll dive deeper into discovering your vein of gold—the strengths, gifts and natural talents you have to give the world.

Practical tips, inspiration and lessons learned from other successful mid-life career changers will help you manifest, create and take practical and inspired steps so you can live your best life. With vision, planning and perseverance, working with purpose, passion and profit can be yours.

Download sample chapters, or purchase Mid-Life Career Rescue:What Makes You Happy from Amazon here >>

Available in paperback and print.

Another important book by Cassandra Gaisford. In the second book of her series, Mid-Life Career Rescue, she gives you the perfect gentle nudge needed to move you forward and make those scary life changes. Ms. Gaisford is like having a life and career coach all wrapped in one by your side. She provides just the right amount of inspiration, motivation, tips and actions to take to get you out of your comfort zone and into the life you deserve. I highly recommend this book for anyone who wants to make a career change but isn't sure how to begin taking steps towards their happiness.

~ **Amazon review**

Get happy now! getBook.at/MakeYouHappy

P.P.S. Be in the know!

If you'd like to be the first to know when other books become available, sign up for my newsletter and receive free giveaways, sneak peeks into new books and helpful tips and strategies to live life more passionately.

ALSO BY CASSANDRA GAISFORD

Mid-Life Career Rescue: The Call for Change

Take the stress out of making a change, confirm your best-fit career and move toward your preferred future.

Available in print and eBook—getBook.at/CareerChange

Mid-Life Career Rescue: What Makes You Happy

Clarify what makes you happy and find your point of brilliance.

Available in print and eBook—getBook.at/MakeYouHappy

Mid-Life Career Rescue: Employ Yourself

Start a business on the side while holding down your job. Or take the leap to self-employed bliss. Choose and grow your own business with confidence. This handy resource will show you how.

Available in print and eBook—getBook.at/EmployYourself

Mid-Life Career Rescue-3 Book Bundle-

Box Set (Books 1-3): The Call for Change, What Makes You Happy, Employ Yourself

More passion, less career groundhog day! Fast-track your success and instantly save $$$ when you buy this bundle of 3 eBook best-sellers.

Available for immediate download—getBook.at/CareerRescueBox

Find Your Passion and Purpose

Focus your energy and time to achieve outstanding personal and professional results. Find your point of brilliance and purpose in life.

Available in print and eBook here—getBook.at/Passion

The Passion-Driven Business Planning Journal:

The Effortless Path to Manifesting Your Business and Career Goals

Are you thinking of starting a business? Would you love to employ yourself but have no idea what to do or how to begin? Or do you have an existing business but yearn for a fresh start? First things first: start from your heart. Your passion-driven business planning journal is the perfect place to begin your love affair.

Available in print and eBook here—viewBook.at/PassionBusinessJournal

Boost Your Self-Esteem and Confidence

Be empowered! Heed the call for greater significance—six easy steps to increase self-confidence, self-esteem, self-value and love yourself more

Available in print and eBook here—

getBook.at/BoostYourSelfEsteemAndConfidence

The Art of Success: Leonardo da Vinci

The 8-Step Blueprint to True Success for Your Relationships, Your Bank Account, Your Body and Your Soul

Leonardo da Vinci had to overcome obstacles to succeed just like you and I. Be inspired by his blueprint for success.

Available in print and eBook here—getBook.at/TheArtofSuccess

The Art of Success: Coco Chanel

The 8-Step Blueprint to True Success for Your Relationships, Your Bank Account, Your Body and Your Soul

Coco Chanel didn't let poverty, rejection, abandonment and fear stop her from pursuing her dream. Talk about rags to riches! Learn her wealth-building secrets and instantly 10X your prosperity and success.

Available in print and eBook here—getBook.at/CocoChanel

The Prosperous Author: Make a Living With Your Writing (Developing a Millionaire Mindset)

In Book One of *The Prosperity for Authors* series, *Developing a Millionaire Mindset*, you'll discover how to create the ultimate mindset for success. Master simple strategies to unlock your potential, overcome the fears that stop you from reaching your fullest potential, fight through your blocks, win your inner creative battles and develop unwavering resilient self-belief.

Although it was written for writers, the principles and strategies can be embraced by business entrepreneurs, actors, dancers, painters, photographers, filmmakers, and thousands of others around the world who want to enhance their mindset and elevate their success.

Available in print and eBook here—*getBook.at/TheProsperousAuthor*

The Prosperous Author: Productivity Hacks: Do Less & Make More

In Book Two of *The Prosperity for Authors series*, getBook.at/AuthorProductivityHacks, you'll learn how to work less and produce more, including powerhouse productivity tools you can harness to help you work smarter not harder, finish what you start, create new books and take them to market so you can sell them faster.

Although it was written for writers, the principles and strategies can be embraced by business entrepreneurs, actors, dancers, painters, photographers, filmmakers, and thousands of others around the world who want to enhance their mindset and elevate their success.

Available here—getBook.at/ProductivityHacks

The Prosperous Author-Two Book Bundle-Box Set (Books 1-2): Developing a Millionaire Mindset, Productivity Hacks: Do Less & Make More: How to Make a Living With Your Writing

Your blueprint for mastering a winning mindset, empowering purposeful productivity, making money and still having fun. By fuelling your desire, empowering your vision, slaying obstacles, mastering your subconscious mind, maintaining optimum health, empowering your relationships, and making a commitment to turn pro, you'll elevate your success.

Available here—getBook.at/ProsperousAuthorBox

The Happy, Healthy Artist: Worry Less, Improve Your Health & Create a Sustainable Creative Career

Brimming with over 40 easy to apply strategies that will boost your mental, emotional and physical well-being, *The Happy, Healthy Artist* is a timeless call to action for anyone who wants to create a sustainable, joyful, writing and creative career.

Available here—viewBook.at/HappyHealthyArtist

Stress Less. Love Life More: How to Stop Worrying, Reduce Anxiety, Eliminate Negative Thinking and Find Happiness

Are you feeling stressed, anxious, overwhelmed and just plain "over it"? Cassandra's newest release may provide the mojo boost you, or someone you love, need. Gain a fresh approach to living, from contemporary quick-fixes to help combat the pressures of modern day-to-day living, to soothing rituals and long-term solutions for a better life. This quintessential lifestyle guide reassures you that joy is within your reach, and shows you how to reclaim your, happiness, health, close relationships, career—and sanity.

Available here—getBook.at/StressLess

Financial Rescue: The Total Money Makeover: Create Wealth, Reduce Debt & Gain Freedom

You may not have the cash at the present moment, and the economy may not be ideal, but that doesn't mean your mind can't be working on your ideas and creating the way to a better future. *Financial Rescue* will show you how to reduce debt and create opportunities in every climate.

Available here—viewBook.at/FinancialRescue

Bounce: Overcoming Adversity, Building Resilience and Finding Joy

Bounce features the most essential and stirring passages from Gaisford's previous books, exploring topics such as meditation, mindfulness, positive health behaviors, and working with fear, depression, anxiety, and other painful emotions.

Bounce encourages a more playful approach to the seriousness of life and the ever-present stressors we all face. Through the course of this book, you will learn practical, creative and simple methods for heightening awareness and overcoming habitual patterns that block happiness and joy and hold you back.

Available here—viewBook.at/Bounce

Sexy Sobriety: Alcohol and Guilt-Free Drinks You'll Love: Easy Recipes for Happier Hours & a Joy-Filled Life

Sexy Sobriety brims with a range of a range of sexy, wonderfully refreshing and healthy alternatives to drinking alcohol.

Cut back or quit drinking entirely without becoming a hermit, being ostracized, or cutting back on an enjoyable social life. These easy to prepare drinks and pre-purchased alcohol-free alternatives can be enjoyed in the privacy of your own home, office party or hip location. "For readers who sincerely want to stop or rescue their drinking, but lack awareness of healthy alcohol-free alternatives, the recipes in this book will pave the way."

Available in print and eBook here—getBook.at/SexySobriety

The Sobriety Journal: The Easy Way to Stop Drinking: The Effortless Path to Being Happy, Healthy and Motivated Without Alcohol

This guided book leaves you free to create your own bespoke journal tailored to support your needs. Includes, Journal Writing Prompts, Empowering and Inspirational Quotes and Recovery Exercises that can be of use in your daily journal writing, working with your sponsor or use in a recovery group. The passion and purpose-inspired *Sobriety Journal* is the perfect place to begin your love affair. Think Brand New You!

Available in print and eBook here—getbook.at/SobrietyJournal

More of Cassandra's practical and inspiring workbooks on a range of career and life enhancing topics can be found on her Amazon Author Page.

Navigate to: https://www.amazon.com/Cassandra-Gaisford/e/B016LGWES2

Newsletters

For inspiring tools and helpful tips subscribe to Cassandra's free newsletters here:

http://www.cassandragaisford.com

Sign up now and receive a free eBook!

FOLLOW YOUR PASSION TO PROSPERITY ONLINE COURSE

I f you need more help to find and live your life purpose you may prefer to take my online course, and watch inspirational and practical videos and other strategies to help you to fulfill your potential.

Follow your passion and purpose to prosperity—online coaching program

Easily discover your passion and purpose, overcoming barriers to success, and create a job or business you love with my self-paced online course.

Gain unlimited lifetime access to this course, for as long as you like—across any and all devices you own. Be supported with practical, inspirational, easy-to-access strategies to achieve your dreams.

To start achieving outstanding personal and professional results with absolute certainty and excitement. **Click here to enroll or find out more— https://the-coaching-lab.teachable.com/p/follow-your-passion-and-purpose-to-prosperity**

ADDITIONAL HELP FROM CASSANDRA

LIFE, CAREER or BUSINESS COACHING

Take your life to the next level!

Cassandra and her team of coaches are available whenever, and for as long as you need. We provide Skype, phone, or email coaching. You can schedule a regular appointment or simply call at times of stress, confusion, or when you just need a motivational kick-start to take your dreams further.

Navigate to: http://www.cassandragaisford.com/coaching/

EMPLOY YOURSELF! TRAIN TO BE A COACH

Is your job stressing you out? Cassandra is passionate about helping people change careers and create businesses they love and still pay the bills! If you share her passion and are seeking work that is fulfilling, financially rewarding and flexible becoming a career and life coach may be just what you have been looking for!

Work with passion and purpose!

Contact us to become an accredited:

- Career coach
- Life coach
- Happy at Work coach
- Creativity coach.

Navigate to: http://www.worklifesolutions.nz/coach-training

ONLINE CERTIFICATION COURSE NOW AVAILABLE

Discover how to make money as a life coach, earn extra income on the side, and easily create your own online business using the Worklife Solutions fail-proof system and attract your first paying client in weeks. All from the comfort of your own home or exotic destination.

Navigate to https://the-coaching-lab.teachable.com/p/worklife-solutions-coach-training-foundation-course

FOLLOW ME AND CONTINUE TO BE INSPIRED

www.facebook.com/cassandra.gaisford
http://twitter.com/cassandraNZ
http://pinterest.com/cassandraNZ
www.youtube.com/user/cassandragaisfordnz

BLOG

Learn more about happiness at work and life by visiting my blog: http://www.cassandragaisford.com/archives/

PRESENTATIONS

For information about products and workshops navigate to here
http://www.cassandragaisford.com/contact/speaking

To ask Cassandra to come and speak at your workplace or conference, contact: cassandra@cassandragaisford.com

NEWSLETTERS

For inspiring tools and helpful tips subscribe to Cassandra's free newsletters here:

http://www.cassandragaisford.com
Sign up now and receive a free eBook!

COACHING OFFER

I'm a woman on a mission.

I'm passionate about passion, joy and helping people stress less and live abundant, prosperous and beautiful love-filled lives. I know from experience this is possible for us all—and I also know from my personal and professional experience that it's hard to achieve on your own.

I love helping people discover their purpose, passion, and potential.

I love guiding people to find their beauty spot—that unique place that resides within us all, where talent, interest, and motivation intersect and enthusiasm collides.

I also adore coaching creative people and helping those with a passion for writing to bring their beautiful books into the world.

I've lived a chameleon life, shaping-shifting to find my place in life. I've had some horror jobs and experiences—and thankfully, some millionaire moments too. With over 25-years professional experience helping people transform their lives, as a holistic psychologist, career counselor, life coach, intuitive and bestselling author of self-empowerment and romance books. . .

. . .if you'd love to live a life of joy, fulfillment, and prosperity you're in good hands.

How we'll take your life to the next level

Often the thing getting in the way of finding your bliss is you! It's hard to step out of what you know or believe you are capable. Your mindset, beliefs and the old scripts that keep running through your head can hold you back. Unchallenged, your limited awareness can keep you, your dreams and your life small.

My strengths, expertise, and joys are awakening a sense of possibility, transforming your mindset, and helping you make the 'impossible' possible through solid, practical and proven strategies, branding and marketing so that you can build yourself a successful business and live the lifestyle you desire.

Whether you:

- Dream of creating a life you're passionate about
- Want to employ yourself or start a business on the side
- Yearn to be more creative
- Would love to write and successfully publish a book
- Fancy a career change and want to build a career you are proud of
- Would love to do what I do and become a transformational life and career coach
- Or just want to take your life to the next level, so you can build yourself a successful business and live the lifestyle you desire...

...you'll be inspired, feel empowered and succeed. Yes, it will take a commitment, but I promise you'll have fun and there will be passion and joy!

As Gary Keller writes in *The One Thing: The Surprisingly Simple Truth Behind Extraordinary Results*, a coach can spur you to better results. "Ideally, a coach can coach you on how to maximise your performance over time. This is how the very best become the very best," says Keller.

Commit to achieving extraordinary results and give your book the best chance possible.

"Thank YOU! Our coaching was immensely helpful, and I have renewed hope for finding my way. You are simply lovely, and brilliant, and wise. So glad our energies aligned, and I found you! I am also so enjoying your books and will give more feedback as I go as well as post reviews online. And they will be GLOWING, I can assure you!"

~ Lisa Webb, artist

"A coaching session with Cassandra is like a light switch to a light bulb. My ideas were there but without that light switch I wasn't able to see them and manifest my dream of running a holistic business from home. Straight away, Cassandra was able to get to the heart of my core values and how to put them into a dream business. I now have the sense of purpose and drive to achieve my business goals. Cassandra's warm personality and positive approach make her a joy to work with. I recommend her to anyone who wants to unlock their personal and professional potential."

~ Shelley Sweeney, writer & Reiki practitioner

Contact me at Cassandra@cassandragaisford.com to find out more. Or navigate to the following page to learn more about my coaching and how it can help you:

http://www.cassandragaisford.com/coaching/

(Did you know that coaching fees are often tax deductible for people who use coaching to improve their business and professional skills? Check with your accountant for details.)

ABOUT THE AUTHOR

Cassandra Gaisford, is a holistic psychologist, award-winning artist, and #1 bestselling author. A corporate escapee, she now lives and works from her idyllic lifestyle property overlooking the Bay of Islands in New Zealand.

Cassandra is best known for the passionate call to redefine what it means to be successful in today's world.

She is a well-known expert in the area of success, passion, purpose and transformational business, career and life change, and is regularly sought after as a keynote speaker, and by media seeking an expert opinion on career and personal development issues.

Cassandra has also contributed to international publications and been interviewed on national radio and television in New Zealand and America.

She has a proven-track record of success helping people find savvy ways to boost their finances, change careers, build a business or become a solopreneur—on a shoestring.

Cassandra's unique blend of business experience and qualifications (BCA, Dip Pych.), creative skills, and well-ness and holistic training (Dip Counselling, Reiki Master Teacher) blends pragmatism and commercial savvy with rare and unique insight and out-of-the-box-thinking for anyone wanting to achieve an extraordinary life.

Learn more about her on her website, her blog, or connect with her on Facebook and Twitter.

FURTHER RESOURCES

Surf The Net

Mathew Johnstone has a wide range of books and resources on mental wellness and mindfulness: www.matthewjohnstone.com.au

www.whatthebleep.com—a powerful and inspiring site emphasizing quantum physics and the transformational power of thought.

www.heartmath.org—comprehensive information and tools help you access your intuitive insight and heart-based knowledge. Validated and supported by science-based research. Check out the additional information about your heart-brain.

Join polymath Tim Ferris and learn from his interesting and informative guests on The Tim Ferris Show http://fourhourworkweek.com/podcast/.

Listen to podcasts which inspire you to become the best version of your writing self—*Joanna Penn's podcast* is very helpful for "author-preneurs" http://www.thecreativepenn.com/podcasts. I also love Neil Patel's podcast for savvy marketing strategies http://neilpatel.com/podcast.

Experience the transformative power of hypnosis. One of my favorite hypnosis sites is the UK-based Uncommon Knowledge. On their website http://www.hypnosisdownloads.com you'll find a range of self-hypnosis mp3 audios, including The Millionaire Mindset program.

Celebrity hypnotherapist and author Marissa Peer is another favorite source of subconscious reprogramming and liberation —www.marisapeer.com.

What beliefs are holding you back? Check out Peer's Youtube clip "How To Teach Your Mind That Everything Is Available To You" here —https://www.youtube.com/watch?v=IKeaAbM2kJg

Enjoy James Clear's fabulous blog content and receive further self-improvement tips based on proven scientific research: http://jamesclear.com/articles

Tim Ferriss recommends a couple of apps for those wanting some help getting started with meditation—Headspace (www.headspace.com) or Calm (www.calm.com).

National Geographic: The Science of Stress: Portrait of a killer
    https://www.youtube.com/watch?v=ZyBsy5SQxqU

Effects of Stress on Your Body
    https://www.youtube.com/watch?v=1p6EeYwp1O4

Mindfulness training

Wellington-based Peter Fernando offers an introductory guided meditation which you can take further. He also meets with individuals and groups in Wellington for philosophical talks on mindfulness and Buddhism. Very enjoyable and great for the soul.
http://www.monthofmindfulness.info

Guided meditations

www.calm.com

Free app with guided meditations

http://eocinstitute.org/meditation/emotional-benefits-of-meditation/
Includes a comprehensive list of the benefits of meditation.

Career Guidance Sites:

www.aarp.org/work - information and tools to help you stay current and connected with what's hot and what's not in today's workplace.

www.lifereimagined.org - loads of inspiration and practical tips to help you maximize your interests and expertise, personalized and interactive.

www.whatthebleep.com – a powerful and inspiring site emphasizing quantum physics and the transformational power of thought.

www.personalitytype.com—created by the authors of *Do What You Are: Discover the Perfect Career for You through the Secrets of Personality*

Type. This site focuses on expanding your awareness of your own type and that of others—including children and partners. This site also contains many useful links.

Books

Master your millionaire mindset with T. Harv Eker's book, *Secrets of the Millionaire Mind: Mastering the Inner Game of Wealth.*

Find your ONE thing with Gary Keller in *The One Thing: The Surprisingly Simple Truth Behind Extraordinary Results.*

Learn from masters in a diverse cross-section of fields—pick up a copy of Tim Ferriss' *Tool of Titans.*

Celebrate being an outlier and learn why clocking up 10,000 hours will help you succeed in Malcolm Gladwell's *Outliers: The Story of Success.*

Struggling in an extroverted world? Introverts are enjoying a renaissance, fueled in part by Susan Cain's terrific bestseller, *Quiet: The Power of Introverts in a World That Can't Stop Talking.*

Copy-cat your way to success with Austin Kleon's great book, *Steal Like An Artist.*

Roll up your sleeves and bring out the big guns to win your creative battle with *The War of Art* by Steven Pressfield.

Power up with a new personality—read Breaking the Habit of Being Yourself: How to Lose Your Mind and Create a New One by Dr. Joe Dispenza.

Unleash the power of your mind by reading *You Are the Placebo: Making Your Mind Matter,* by Dr. Joe Dispenza.

Manifest your prosperity with Rhonda Byrne in her popular book, *The Secret.*

Ensure you don't starve by reading Jeff Goins collated wisdom in *Real Artists Don't Starve: Timeless Strategies for Thriving in the New Creative Age.*

Fortify your faith with Julia Cameron's book, *Faith and Will.*

How to Survive and Thrive in Any Life Crisis, Dr. Al Siebert

Thrive: The Third Metric to Redefining Success and Creating a Happier Life, Arianna Huffington

(This book has great content throughout and some excellent resources listed in the back.)

The Power of Now: A Guide to Spiritual Enlightenment, Eckhart Tolle

The Book of Joy, The Dalai Lama and Archbishop Desmond Tutu

The Sleep Revolution: Transforming Your Life One Night at a Time, Arianna Huffington

Quiet the Mind: An Illustrated Guide on How to Meditate, Mathew Johnstone

Comfortable with Uncertainty: 108 Teachings on Cultivating Fearlessness and Compassion, Pema Chodron

Power vs. Force: The Hidden Determinants of Human Behavior, David R. Hawkins

Learn how to live an inspired life with Tarot cards and other oracles. Read Jessa Crispin's book, *The Creative Tarot: A Modern Guide to an Inspired Life.*

Check out all of Collette-Baron-Reid's books, including: *Uncharted: The Journey Through Uncertainty to Infinite Possibility* and *Messages from Spirit: The Extraordinary Power of Oracles, Omens, and Signs.*

ABOUT THE AUTHOR

Cassandra Gaisford, is a holistic psychologist, award-winning artist, and #1 bestselling author. A corporate escapee, she now lives and works from her idyllic lifestyle property overlooking the Bay of Islands in New Zealand.

Cassandra is best known for the passionate call to redefine what it means to be successful in today's world.

She is a well-known expert in the area of success, passion, purpose and transformational business, career and life change, and is regularly sought after as a keynote speaker, and by media seeking an expert opinion on career and personal development issues.

Cassandra has also contributed to international publications and been interviewed on national radio and television in New Zealand and America.

She has a proven-track record of success helping people find savvy ways to boost their finances, change careers, build a business or become a solopreneur—on a shoestring.

Cassandra's unique blend of business experience and qualifications (BCA, Dip Pych.), creative skills, and well-ness and holistic training (Dip Counselling, Reiki Master Teacher) blends pragmatism and commercial savvy with rare and unique insight and out-of-the-box-thinking for anyone wanting to achieve an extraordinary life.

Learn more about her on her website, her blog, or connect with her on Facebook and Twitter.

STAY IN TOUCH

FOLLOW ME AND CONTINUE TO BE INSPIRED

www.cassandragaisford.com
www.twitter.com/cassandraNZ
www.instagram.com/cassandragaisford
www.facebook.com/cassandra.gaisford
http://www.youtube.com/cassandragaisfordnz
https://www.pinterest.com/cassandraNZ
www.linkedin.com/in/cassandragaisford

BLOG

Be inspired by regular posts to help you follow your bliss, slay self-doubt, and sustain healthy habits. You'll find a variety of articles and tips about people pursuing their passion and strategies to help you pursue yours—personally and professionally.

http://www.cassandragaisford.com

PRESENTATIONS

For information about products and workshops navigate to here www.cassandragaisford.com/contact/speaking

To ask Cassandra to come and speak at your workplace or conference, contact: cassandra@cassandragaisford.com

ACKNOWLEDGMENTS

This book (and my new life) was made possible by the amazing generosity, open heartedness, and wonderful friendship of so many people. Thank you!

Sir Edmund Hillary often said that even Mount Everest wasn't climbed alone. A great achievement, or in my case a good book, is a product of collaboration. This project has, at times, loomed larger than the highest mountain in the world. I could not have persevered without the tremendous encouragement from a wealth of supportive and talented people.

To all the amazingly interesting clients who have allowed me to help them over the years, and to the wonderful people who read my newspaper columns and wrote to me with their stories of reinvention —thank you. Your feedback, deep sharing, requests for help, and inspired, courageous action continues to inspire me.

I'd also like to say a special thanks to the staff at *The Dominion Post* newspaper who gave me my first break into published writing. This book would never have existed had they not acted on my suggestion that a careers column would be a great idea. For over four years they gave me the encouragement and artistic freedom to write freely on a range of topics—all with the goal of helping encourage and inspire others.

I'm also grateful to the Health Editor of *Marie Claire* magazine whom, after she had accepted a short article, said I had the bones of a good book and should write it.

My thanks also to my terrific friends and supporters. And, of course, I can never say thank you enough to my family, particularly my parents and grandparents, who have instilled me with such tremendous values and life skills.

My daughter, Hannah—I wish for you everything that your heart desires. Without you, I doubt I would ever have accomplished all the things I have in my life.

Thank you.

PLEASE LEAVE A REVIEW

Your feedback encourages and sustains me, and I love hearing from you.

Show your support. Share how this book has helped you by leaving a REVIEW—Even a one-liner would be helpful.

I recently received an email from a reader who said, *"Your books are a fantastic resource and until now I never even thought to write a review. Going forward I will be reviewing more books. So many great ones out there and I want to support the amazing people that write them."*

Great reviews also help people find good books.

Thank you

PS: If you enjoyed this book, do me a small favor to help spread the word about it and share links to purchase this book on Facebook, Twitter and other social networks.

COPYRIGHT

Published by Blue Giraffe Publishing 2017
   Blue Giraffe Publishing is a division of Worklife Solutions Ltd.
www.worklifesolutions.nz

For orders, please email: info@worklifesolutions.co.nz
   See   our   complete   catalogue   on   Amazon   at
Author.to/CassandraGaisford and www.cassandragaisford.com
   ISBN Print 978-0-9941484-3-8
   ISBN Ebook 978-0-9951072-0-5
   First Edition

EXCERPT:MIND OVER MOJITOS: HOW MODERATING YOUR DRINKING CAN CHANGE YOUR LIFE

BONUS: ALCOHOL-FREE DRINKS YOU'LL LOVE

Do you drink too much? Take back control. Stop drinking now without missing out on the fun with easy alcohol-free alternatives.

ENJOY this carefully curated selection from my book, *Mind Over Mojitos: How Moderating Your Drinking Can Change Your Life*

Available in eBook and paperback here —viewBook.at/MindOverMojitosRecipes

CASSANDRA GAISFORD

MIND
OVER
MOJITOS

How Moderating Your Drinking
Can Change Your Life

Easy Alcohol-Free
Recipes for Happier
Hours & a Joy Filled Life

Bestselling author of Stress Less, Love Life More

CONTENTS

EXCERPT:MIND OVER MOJITOS: HOW MODERATING YOUR DRINKING CAN CHANGE YOUR LIFE

PART I

PRAISE FOR MIND YOUR MOJITOS

"Anyone who needs to cut back their drinking, be kept on track or inspired will find genuine help in this honest, insightful book."

~ CS Sloan, counselor

"More motivating inspiration from Cassandra. Be honest with yourself ... do you drink too much? Do you want to take back the control that alcohol has over you? Cassandra shows you how you can do this without missing out on the fun. Complete abstinence does not have to be the answer, neither does drinking water in boring tumblers at social functions have to be subject to questioning peers.

As the daughter of an alcoholic father, I am well aware of my own predisposition. When he fought for control, he would drink orange juice on ice, in a highball glass with a splash of soda and a wedge of orange. It looked just like a Screwdriver and no-one ever questioned it.

With Cassandra's advice and delicious mocktail recipes, you too can release the grip of alcohol and regain your life."

~ Niki Firth, Amazon Review

"Geared toward problem drinkers struggling to cut back or quit drinking as well as those who want to be reinspired during recovery, this book helps those looking for alternatives to alcohol to take pleasure in booze-free alternatives... For readers who sincerely want to stop drinking the recipes in this book will pave the way."

~ L. Wells, Director

"Great Writer. Great Recipes. Pleasantly surprised by the quality of writing and the inventiveness of the recipes."

~ Amazon 5-star Review

AUTHOR'S NOTE

"The world is not dangerous because of those who do harm but because of those who look at it without doing anything."

~ Albert Einstein, genius

December 2016—the year I took control of my drinking. Perhaps like you, I'd grown concerned about how much, and how regularly, I was consuming alcohol.

I knew the side-effects, and I didn't like them—insomnia, depression, aggression, muddled thinking, bloating, weight gain and more. But still, I couldn't control alcohol.

One month of sobriety was the longest time I'd ever managed.

I tried reading books, used self-hypnosis, made a star-chart and ticked off my alcohol-free days. There were two ticks one week, none the next, then some longer stretches. But, despite my positive intentions and extraordinary will, booze always reigned victoriously.

Nothing worked.

Until Christmas 2016 when I finally got angry—and scared—

enough to make a change. To protect others' privacy I won't go into detail, suffice to say that my turning point involved a rifle, shots fired and fearing for my life.

But my motivation and my personal story of alcohol being in control began earlier than that. My grandmother was an alcoholic. And her father before that—and both their stories, like many people affected by alcohol was one of tragedy.

In the 1930's one drunken brawl outside the local pub in New Zealand left one man dead and my great-grandfather charged with murder.

My grandmother was four, and her brother aged six when they were taken into foster care. They never saw their mother, father or each other again.

Their story, my story, your story is a far too common one.

For many people complete removal of alcohol is the only cure. Western culture does not make it easy—happiness, we are lead to believe, can only be found in a bottle. Changing this mistaken belief is one of the reasons I have written this book.

Mindful drinking

Mind Over Mojitos is not an anti-alcohol book. It offers a fresh approach, encouraging you to view your relationship to alcohol more mindfully and offering you some tasty booze-free alternatives.

While it's important to highlight the dangers of drinking too much, my aim is to highlight the life-changing benefits of drinking far less.

Importantly, I'll share some simple but effective ways to mix, mingle and practice sober socialising—and still feel great.

A fresh approach

Drinking too much is a culturally sanctioned, actively encouraged "cure" for the *dis-ease* of modern life. Except it isn't a cure at all. It's not a sustainable quick fix. Many people are using alcohol, consciously or unconsciously, to self-medicate all or some of the following:

- Stress
- Anxiety
- Depression
- Low self-esteem
- Sexual Abuse
- Trauma
- Shame
- Guilt
- Boredom

There is a cure

Many people who have battled alcohol dependency and addiction overcame obstacles just like you and I. But the single biggest factor was their ability to take control of their drinking.

Sometimes they deferred to experts. Sometimes they turned to God. Sometimes they joined a support group, or they embraced spontaneous sobriety and went it alone.

But the one thing they all had in common was the knowledge that their drinking was taking more than it was giving.

In every instance, when people nailed their drink demons, they universally agreed that their life was more beautiful sober.

"I gave up alcohol in 1980. I enjoyed it far too much, to the point where I frequently got intoxicated. Everything in my life changed for the better stopped. It was the right decision," said the medical doctor and self-empowerment author Deepak Chopra.

Why I wrote this book

The successful pursuit of sobriety is born from my own experience, both professionally as a holistic psychologist, and personally as a woman with a genetic predisposition to alcoholism. My desire and determination to liberate others from the clutches of booze inspired this book.

During a recent interview I was asked: 'What do you hope readers get out of *Mind Over Mojitos?* My response was "choice."

If I can help people gain new knowledge, enhance their awareness and fall in love with booze-free alternatives then *Mind Over Mojitos* has made an important and much-needed contribution.

My hope is that *Mind Over Mojito's* easy recipes for happier hours & healthier, joy-filled living will help you achieve your goals—whether that's getting sober or just cutting back—and create positive, permanent transformational change in your life. And that one day, should our paths cross, you will tell me that your life truly is more beautiful sober.

Who Is This Book For?

If you want to control your drinking and live a happier, healthier life on your own terms, this book is for you.

For readers who sincerely want to stop or rescue their drinking, but lack awareness of healthy alcohol-free alternatives, the recipes in this book will pave the way.

If you're a heavy drinker or love someone who is, *Mind Over Mojitos: How Moderating Your Drinking Can Change Your Life* will provide healthy alternatives to drinking alcohol that will empower the journey to wellness and happiness.

Or, you might just want to inspire others and lead the way by controlling alcohol, either by cutting back or giving up completely *Mind Over Mojitos* will come to your rescue.

Mind Over Mojitos: How Moderating Your Drinking Can Change Your Life, will help you:

- Take control of your drinking
- Relieve stress and still have fun
- Enjoy the taste of sexy and healthy alcohol-free alternatives

- Eliminate alcohol to do a life and career reset
- Love drinking minus the booze, hangover, and guilt
- Join the trend toward tantalizing tee-totaling
- Enjoy happier hours
- Improve your relationships
- Live a joy-filled healthier life.

As fellow New Zealand psychologist and television personality Nigel Latta says, "It's also interesting, don't you think, that given the alcohol industry thinks education is so important, their contribution to 'education' of the public is so... well... limp. They don't even bother to put any real resources into 'education' even though they say it will make a difference."

This was my motivation for writing this book, and for sharing the recipes that have worked for me, my friends and family and my clients in the quest for sobriety.

We have to be the change we want to see. Part of this involves passing on to others the knowledge that I've learned.

My hope is that you step into living sober joyfully. Despite any trepidation, fear or worry, you may feel, my wish is that you'll discover that learning to control alcohol is a pleasure that you never forget to enjoy.

BLAME YOUR BRAIN?

Why do we over-drink? The answer, some neuroscientists believe, lies not in our bellies, but in our brains.

A team of New Zealand scientists has recently begun a new study that aims to pinpoint a 'sensory fingerprint' behind the urge to eat for pleasure. Their findings appear to apply equally to alcohol.

"Eating (and drinking) is a multi-sensory experience, where the taste, smell, appearance and even sound of food are integrated to give pleasure," says Dr. Mei Peng, of Otago University's Department of Food Science.

Some people are particularly susceptible to eating (and drinking) for pleasure, or what's termed hedonic pleasure, says Peng. These differences are thought to be related to brain networks related to rewards, add alcohol to the mix and this makes fighting against our desire to over-indulge a challenging task.

But we can trick our brains and stimulate the reward networks by losing the booze, and plying ourselves with all the other sensory inputs which alcohol barons know make us attracted and addicted to their products. Things like bright, tantalizing colors; sensuously delicious smells; sparkling water bubbling over cool crystal; the warm, sultry feel of a well-rounded glass, cupped in your hand, simultaneously warming your drink.

Plus, alcohol is basically sugar, with more kilojoules. We know how addictive sugar is, but this time we'll get a natural high with plenty of fruits and no booze—and no poisonous ethanol (the ingredient found in beer, wine and spirits that causes drunkness and destroys your brain cells.)

Instead of pickled pretend prettiness you'll reap the benefits of mindful sobriety and beat the drug barons at their own game. Fun!

ABOUT THESE RECIPES

Organized into two volumes, Spring/Summer, and Fall/Winter, this book is a series of carefully curated fun and healthy alcohol alternatives. *Mind Over Mojitos* guides you through a variety of different mock-tail recipes and booze-free alternatives that will make your tastebuds sing and send your dopamine levels soaring.

I've chosen a range of wonderfully refreshing drinks, particularly during the summertime, which are great for picnics or barbeques or just enjoying around the home. Many contain seasonal fruits and berries, are thirst-quenching and also pack some vitamins. Perfect for people who don't like drinking or are not of legal drinking age.

There are two kinds of wintery yet festive drinks to guzzle during the cooler seasons: sparkly and fun mixes that utilize winter fruit, and those that are warm and cozy.

Enjoy this selection, or channel your own mixologist and create your own.

Don't forget, if you ever find yourself in a bar and at a loss for what to drink, or you want to fit in, simply ask for a mocktail (which is what I did when I got the bar staff to create the Virgin Island Fox recipe in this book). Or order a look-alike drink in a fancy glass.

Voila! You'll blend in without having to give everyone a lengthy spiel or justify why you're not drinking alcohol.

Be prepared—plan your booze-free alternative ahead of time and you'll never default to drinking alcohol simply because there was nothing else.

If you create something tasty please share in the dedicated Facebook group where you'll find plenty of thirsty booze-free devotees —https://www.facebook.com/YourBeautifulMindControlAlcoholBoo k

Drinking a non-alcoholic drink should be a fun, sensual and pleasurable experience. Before we dive deeper into some luscious recipes lets clarify what I mean by sobriety, remind yourself of why you need to lose the booze, and then look at the importance of giving good glass. And yes, we will have fun!

WHAT IS SOBRIETY?

Sobriety is more than being teetotal. It's more than fighting a daily battle with your willpower. It's more than the number of drinks you do, or don't knockback.

Sobriety actually means not drinking alcohol in excess, being intoxicated, or drunk.

Dictionary.com defines sobriety as, "the state or quality of being sober; temperance or moderation, especially in the use of alcoholic beverages."

Sobriety does NOT mean abstinence, as some organizations like Alcoholics Anonymous take it to mean.

"'Sobriety' is a word whose 12-step misuse now pervades our entire culture, along with ruining addiction treatment," says addiction expert Dr. Stanton Peele.

"In fact, the DSM psychiatric manual, unbeknownst to virtually everyone who uses it, including even experts who write about it, contains no abstinence criterion for recovery (actually called remission)," Stanton says.

The real issue to focus on is addiction—something, along with dependence, I explore in my book *Your Beautiful Mind: Control Alcohol, Discover Freedom, Find Happiness and Change Your Life*—integrating neuroscience, cognitive therapy, proven tools and teachings to help people suffering from alcohol dependence and addiction win the battle.

Sobriety is about controlling alcohol and living life on your terms.

Mind Over Mojitos and the enticing alcohol-free drink recipes in this book will empower and enable you to more easily make positive choices again and again.

Let's look at why sobriety is sexy and what living sober will do for you.

YOU BOOZE, YOU LOSE

Many people mistakenly believe drinking alcohol will increase their happiness. But alcohol is a depressant and in large quantities is draining on your body and mind.

Experience may have already taught you that too much booze muddles the mind, ignites aggression, reduces responsiveness, and ultimately depresses.

It's also hard to quit—alcohol is one of the most addictive legalized drugs on the planet.

It's also a well-documented neurotoxin—a toxic substance that inhibits, damages, and destroys the cells and tissues of your nervous system.

To bounce back from depression, anxiety and stress many people limit their drinking or consciously decide not to touch a drop. Keeping their resolve often takes extraordinary willpower.

Author and public speaker Deepak Chopra gave up drinking. "I liked it too much," he once said. Steven King, after almost losing his family and destroying his writing career, managed to quit.

Other people like Amy Winehouse devastatingly never made it. At only 27, she died of alcohol poisoning in 2011.

The risk of suicide also increases for stressed people who turn to drink. As I've already discussed, alcohol abuse and excessive drinking is a major cause of anxiety and depression, impairs mental reasoning and critical thinking—increasing the likelihood of making tragic and often impulsive choices.

Risking destroying your career, ruining your relationships, sacrificing your sanity, and in the extreme, taking your life, is a massive price to pay for a mistaken belief that to be happy, or to numb your anxiety, or cope with stress you need to drink more booze.

Bounce beautifully through life by exploring your relationship to drink and approaching it more mindfully.

If you're not in the mood to quit for good consider a period of sobriety. Instead of focusing on what you may be giving up, turn your mind to what you may gain—a better, more energized version of yourself.

Mind Over Mojitos will inspire your quest for success. Let's take a closer look at the growing trend and life-changing magic of mindful drinking.

MINDFUL DRINKING

"*No Beers, Who Cares (BWC) isn't about making anyone feel bad about drinking. It's a movement towards shifting attitudes around how and why we drink, and helping people become more aware of their beliefs and habits and having a freaking good time doing so.*"

~ Claire Robbie, founder No Beers, Who Cares

ROBBIE DESCRIBES HER NO BEERS, Who Cares initiative as not anti-alcohol, but as a pro-mindfulness initiative.

"There's a shift around the world as people understand how incredible life can be without drinking and it's time to bring that high vibration to New Zealand," Robbie (Jack & Olive Retreats, yoga/meditation teacher and journalist) says, "and it's an amazing step towards living more mindfully."

Claire Robbie was a news reporter on TV3's Nightline before a tumultuous time led her to discover the life-changing benefits of yoga and mediation and life without alcohol. At a low point in her life, what started as a hobby became an essential part of her healing process, and as her love for her new practices grew, so did the sense that she had discovered a new vocation.

NBWC isn't about making anyone feel bad about drinking. It's a movement towards shifting attitudes around how and why we drink, and helping people become more aware of their beliefs and habits and having an awesome time doing so. The focus is less about giving something up, but boosting your awareness of how much you gain.

"What we've seen is that giving up alcohol is a keystone habit. A keystone habit is one that unlocks your full well-being potential. Just a few of the benefits of going alcohol-free such as extra energy, motivation, vitality, productivity, money, and time, will begin to pave the way to the life you have always dreamed of," Robbie says.

How can you approach alcohol more mindfully? What might you be giving up by going alcohol free? How much might you gain?

What are you prepared to change in your life? What would stop you? Read on for further incentives on why sobriety is good for you.

WHAT CAN SOBRIETY DO?

M any people struggle to control alcohol because they're not motivated by sobriety. But being sober isn't just about not drinking.

Sobriety is achieved by putting energy and effort toward something you really desire. It's not about saying 'no' to alcohol, and more about saying 'yes!' to living a beautiful life.

There's nothing sexy about drinking too much, slurring your words, staggering around 'legless' or being angrily argumentative. And it's definitely not sexy to puke over yourself, or end up shagging a stranger because you've drunk way too much.

Why do you want to control your drinking?

Knowing why you want something is just as important as knowing what you want.

The many benefits of reducing your alcohol intake, or not drinking at all, include:

✓ A stronger ability to focus on your goals and dreams
✓ Improved confidence and self-esteem
✓ Increased productivity
✓ Increased memory, mental performance, and decision-making
✓ Better control of your emotions

✓ Sweeter relationships

✓ Greater intuition and spiritual intelligence

✓ Authentic happiness

✓ Improved finances

✓ Reduces dehydration and slows down the aging process—making you look and feel sexier for longer!

NOT EVERYONE BATTLES WITH BOOZE. Whether you cut back or eliminate alcohol entirely, the choice is ultimately yours. Only you know the benefits alcohol delivers or the success it destroys. But I'm guessing because you're attracted to this book you're motivated to live happier hours and kick the alcohol habit easily.

Before we take a deep dive into some delicious booze-free recipes, let's take a look at the psychological and sensory benefits of choosing the right glass. If it looks like alcohol, and it's not alcohol you'll be less stressed by peer-pressure to drink and you'll still feel sophisticated.

GIVING GOOD GLASS

Remember it's all in the glass—be sure to pour your drinks into something nice. Drinking a non-alcoholic drink should be a pleasurable experience, and presentation and pleasure go hand-in-hand.

Check out this list below and learn more about the scientific and psychological reasons that it's important to be choosy about your glass.

- The elegance of certain glasses (can give individuals a perception of a finer drinking experience
- The shape of your glass can affect how much and how quickly you drink
- Different glasses bring out the aromas and flavors
- Tall, tapered shapes capture the carbonation and color; glasses with wider bases allows room for swirling to release aromas, which then get trapped at the narrow top. A rounded bottom makes it easy to cup in your hand, simultaneously warming your drink.
- A martini glass's cone shape prevents your ingredients from separating. The long stem also ensures your hands

won't affect the temperature of the drink. As a bonus, the martini glass is sexy no matter who's holding it!

- Champagne coupes, the champagne flutes of our grandparents' generation look elegant, plus the stem keeps your drink cool
- The highball glass is ideal for carbonated mocktails. It's best to keep less surface liquid exposed to air—the more exposed, the quicker the carbonation will evaporate, leaving you with a flat drink.
- Lowball glasses are ideal for high-intensity drinks served on the rocks because they average two to four ounces. Nice since drinking a two-ounce mocktail in a 10-ounce highball may feel a little weak.
- Tulip or white wine glass. Small, slender, tulip-shaped glassware, help slow down any rise in temperature from the chilled beverages, while the stem of the glass allows you to hold your drink without your hands heating it up—keeping your drink cooler for longer.
- Warmer drinks should be served in larger, bowl-shaped glasses to increase surface area and allow for more aroma release.
- Tulip champagne flutes. The narrow, tulip-shaped flute is a familiar drinking vessel at weddings and toast-worthy occasions for holding your celebratory bubbly. The carbonation is the major reason behind the shape. The glass helps retain Champagne's trademark carbonation, and the bowl is also designed to visually highlight the rising bubbles. Perfect for non-alcoholic champagne mixes and carbonated drinks with fizz.
- Stemless glass. With their clean design and easy-to-clean shape (no worries about shattering a delicate stem here!), stemless glasses are best for drinks served at room temp since your hands holding the glass can unintentionally heat up cooler drinks.

Size matters! Small can be beautiful. A tiny crystal long stemmed-glass is one of my favorite glasses to enjoy a wee sip of beer or wine on special occasions. Remember sobriety is not about abstinence but about being in control of your drinking.

But, with so many tasty alternatives to booze, you'll soon find, as I did, that you'll kick the drink habit easily.

Are you ready to discover easy recipes for happier hours of joy-filled sober living? Part One starts with spring and summer, alcohol-free alternatives to enjoy. Recipes for the cooler months follows in Part Two.

First up, my personal favorite—Virgin Island Fox!

PART I

NON-ALCOHOLIC DRINKS FOR SPRING & SUMMER

1

VIRGIN ISLAND FOX

A mocktail version of a classic created for me by the hip-cool folk at Charlotte's Kitchen in Pahia, The Bay of Islands, New Zealand—my spiritual home. An elegant and restrained cocktail with subtle richness balanced with lovely zest.

INGREDIENTS

- 1 tsp orange marmalade
- 90mls grapefruit juice
- 30mls lime juice
- 15 mls sugar syrup
- Ice

METHOD

- Add all ingredients except the ice into a mixer

- Single strain over ice into a wine glass
- Garnish – grapefruit

PASSION FRUIT BUBBLY

G uilt-free sparkle when passion fruit is in season and mixed with sparkling wine for a festive drink.

INGREDIENTS

- 1/2 Lemon, juice of
- 1 small bunch of mint
- 2 cups caster sugar
- 1/2 tsp Salt
- 1 cup of ice
- 1 bottle sparkling wine or soda water
- 2 cups water
- 1 tsp citric acid
- 1 cup of passion fruit pulp (fresh or tinned)

Method

- Place all the ingredients in a saucepan and stir over a medium heat until the sugar is dissolved

- Bring to the boil, take of the heat and allow to cool
- Taste to see if the cordial needs some extra lemon juice
- Serve I part cordial to 3 parts bubbly over lots of ice and garnish with fresh mint
- Keep any leftover cordial in a clean and airtight container, refrigerated for up to 4 weeks
- Makes about 750ml of cordial

3

PASSION FRUIT POWER PUNCH

Perfect for a hot day and easy to mix. Displays aromas of bright fruit and hints of citrus. Rich texture and a sparkling twist. Finishes just like an Indian Summer—long and lovely.

INGREDIENTS

- 1 cup of passion fruit pulp (fresh or tinned)
- I good handful of mint leaves (plus extras to serve)
- I squeezed lime (1 lime per 4 drinks)
- I cup of sparkling water per drink

METHOD

Combine passion fruit, lime juice and mint over ice and then top with sparkling water. Serve with extra mint in the glass.

4

BLUEBERRY AND MAPLE MOJITO

S tunning and stimulating! Exotic in style, clean and crisp, zesty on the palate with aromas of mint and limes. A complete winner and sure to impress even the most discerning drinker.

INGREDIENTS

- 8-10 mint leaves, plus more for garnish
- 1 tsp fresh lime juice
- 1 tbsp. good-quality maple syrup
- 1/3 cup organic blueberry juice-no added sugar
- 1/2 cup soda
- Frozen blueberries, for garnish

METHOD

ADD the mint leaves to a glass (size depends on how much you want). Muddle well until the mint releases its flavor.

Add the lime juice, maple syrup, blueberry juice and soda to the glass and stir until all the ingredients are well-combined.

SERVES 1, prep time 5 minutes

5

TAMARILLO THYME SPRITZER

This zesty drink created by my partner, Lorenzo, ticks all the right boxes—quirky, original and something completely different. A delicious drink that sits perfectly in the long lazy days of our new world New Zealand summer. More than flavor it smells good too.

INGREDIENTS

- 3 organic tamarillo (tree tomato)
- Soda water
- I tsp brown sugar
- Sprigs of thyme

METHOD

COMBINE CRUSHED tamarillo and thyme with brown sugar over ice and then top with sparkling water. Serve with extra thyme in the glass.

6

VIRGIN STRAWBERRY DAIQUIRI

When it's summertime the strawberries are easy! Here are a few yummy recipes for virgin strawberry daiquiris. The berries are thirst-quenching and also pack vivacious vitamins. The palate is mouth-watering and intense from the very first sip right through to the finish.

INGREDIENTS

- 1 ounce of fresh lime juice
- 3 ounces of fresh strawberries
- 2 teaspoons of sugar (or more if the strawberries are tart)
- Cracked ice

METHOD

- Fill your blender with the cracked ice. Add the lime juice, strawberries and sugar and blend until completely smooth.

- If the mixture is too thick, add a little water.
- When you're finished, pour the drink into a chilled glass and garnish it with a fresh strawberry.

Virgin Daiquiri with Soda

Ingredients

- 2 large strawberries without the tops
- 1/4 cup sugar
- 1 tablespoon of lime juice
- 3/4 cup of lemon-lime soda, such as 7-UP or Sprite
- 4 medium ice cubes

Instructions

- In a blender, blend the strawberries, sugar, lime juice, and lemon-lime soda.
- Add the ice cubes and blend all the ingredients until they are smooth. If the drink is too thick, add more soda.

7

GRAPEFRUIT HONEY GINGER SODA

L ight and tangy fizz, sweetened with honey, not sugar, and a hint
of ginger provides a note of warmth in cooler months.

This recipe is for a syrup that you can mix with carbonated water
(store-bought or homemade). It has a bittersweet, grown-up flavor
from the use of grapefruit zest and a slight spiciness from the addition of fresh ginger.

INGREDIENTS

- Zest of 1 large pink or red grapefruit (preferably organic)
- 1 cup freshly-squeezed pink or red grapefruit juice (from about 1 large grapefruit; if necessary, top off with water to make 1 cup
- 3/4 cup mild-flavored honey
- 1/4 cup chopped fresh ginger
- Carbonated water, for serving

METHOD

COMBINE THE GRAPEFRUIT ZEST, grapefruit juice, honey, and ginger in a small saucepan over medium heat. Boil for 2 minutes, stirring to dissolve the honey.

Remove from heat and let cool. Strain the syrup through a sieve into a clean container and discard the solids.

To serve, spoon 2 tablespoons of syrup into an 8-ounce glass, top with carbonated water, and stir to combine. Taste and add more syrup, if desired.

The syrup can be refrigerated for up to 1 week.

Looking beyond soda, the syrup can also be used in cocktails or drizzled over fresh fruit salad.

SOURCE:

https://www.thekitchn.com/recipe-grapefruit-ginger-honey-soda-syrup-recipes-from-the-kitchn-198705

8

THE MEG RYAN: A BRIGHT & BUBBLY
BLENDED BERRY DRINK

Y ou will love this drink—just like one of the world's most adored actresses. A fun, frivolous, fantastic winner. Pure delight.

INGREDIENTS

- 1 cup berries (whatever is in season)
- 1 tsp lemon juice
- 2 tbsp honey
- 1 cup soda water

METHOD

ADD BERRIES, lemon juice, and honey to a blender and combine until smooth. Add soda water and pulse until combined. If using frozen berries, you may add ingredients all at once, but you might need to add a dash of soda water at the end to bubble things back up to our tongue tingling standards.

That's all there is to it, nothing fancy, nothing shaken, nothing stirred and nothing strained (unless you really, really want to). Make sure to pulse some water through your blender when done so clean up is extra easy and you don't even have to worry about dishes. All you'll have left to do is frolic around looking fabulous and smiling making people everywhere love you. Seriously, the drink has powers!

SOURCE:

https://www.thekitchn.com/recipe-a-bright-bubbly-blended-124969

9

PINEAPPLE CHAMOMILE TEA

Refreshing, calming and restorative—what's not to love about this nifty, nerve-enhancing mix. A luminous golden glow in a glass, layered with chamomile and honey to finish. Enjoy!

INGREDIENTS

- 4 Chamomile tea bags
- 1 1/2 cups of water
- 1/2 cup frozen pineapple chunks
- 2 1/2 cups crushed ice
- 2 tablespoon chopped basil
- Honey, to taste

METHOD

BOIL THE WATER in a small saucepan. Remove the pan from the heat, add the tea bags and steep them for 2-3 minutes. Allow the tea to cool.

Add the cooled tea, 1 cup of the ice, the pineapple, and the honey to a blender and blend together. Stir in the basil leaves. (It will be frothy so let it sit for a couple minutes so the contents of the blender can settle. The longer you let the flavors come together the better the tea will taste.

Evenly fill two glasses with the rest of the crushed ice, and pour the tea over. Serve!

SOURCE:

http://chocolateforbasil.com/pineapple-chamomile-tea/

10

VIRGIN MOJITO

E asy to mix and a refreshing to drink on a simmering hot day. Fresh, bright and crisp. Feel the love in this powerful, tight and elegant perennial favorite. Wow!

INGREDIENTS

- 1/3 cup Apple juice
- 1/3 cup Sparkling water
- 1 whole lime, sliced and quartered
- 3 mint leaves
- 1 teaspoon sugar

METHOD

- Muddle the lime, sugar and mint leaves until they are just releasing the juice

- Place ice in a glass, add muddled mixture and pour in apple juice
- Top with sparkling water and stir
- Garnish with a slice of lime and mint leaf and serve

SOURCE:
https://www.soberjulie.com/2016/06/mojito-recipe/

DID YOU ENJOY THIS EXCERPT?

ENJOY this carefully curated selection from my book, *Mind Over Mojitos: How Moderating Your Drinking Can Change Your Life*
Available in eBook and paperback here —viewBook.at/MindOverMojitosRecipes

70087612R00202

Made in the USA
San Bernardino, CA
24 February 2018